Care for the Dying

Care for the Dying

A Practical and Pastoral Guide

Sioned Evans
and
Andrew Davison

CASCADE *Books* · Eugene, Oregon

CARE FOR THE DYING
A Practical and Pastoral Guide

First published in the UK in 2013 by the Canterbury Press Norwich,
Hymns Ancient and Modern Ltd., 3rd Floor, Invicta House, 108–114
Golden Lane, London, EC1Y 0TG

Cascade Books
An Imprint of Wipf and Stock Publishers
199 W. 8th Ave., Suite 3
Eugene, OR 97401

www.wipfandstock.com

ISBN 13: 978-1-62564-802-0

Cataloguing-in-Publication data:

Davison, Andrew, 1974–

Care for the dying : a practical and pastoral guide / Sioned Evans and
Davison.

xvi + 254 pp. ; 23 cm. Includes bibliographical references.

ISBN 13: 978-1-62564-802-0

1. Death—Religious aspects—Christianity. 2. Terminal care. 3. Palliative care—methods. 4. Death—Moral and ethical aspects. I. Evans, Sioned.
II. Title.

BT825 D38 2014

Contents

The Westcott Foundation

Westcott House is an Anglican theological college in the heart of Cambridge, England. Through the Westcott Foundation it seeks to serve the wider Church, supporting and inspiring those engaged in public ministry. It has two particular aims: first, to contribute to the continuing ministerial development of ordained and lay leaders in the Church of England, and second, to provide well-researched, strategic and timely theological resources on matters of public concern for those engaged in Church leadership. *Care for the Dying* is the first book published by the Foundation in collaboration with Canterbury Press.

Acknowledgements

Sioned Evans: The material for this book would never have arisen without the learning I have gained from my many teachers; those members of the palliative care teams I have worked with who taught me how to be a palliative care doctor and the patients who continue to teach me. I would like to thank Rebecca Whitehead for initially encouraging me to write. Many people came forward with articles, experiences and suggestions for the book. Of note I would like to thank Trevor Jameson, Professor Peter Roebuck, the Revd Samantha Stayte, the Revd Jackie Bullen, the Revd Ruth Bond and Ruth Springer. I tapped into the knowledge of experienced hospice and hospital chaplains and I am very grateful for the insights of the Revd John Spencer, who was the first hospice chaplain I worked with, the Revd Dr Andrew Goodhead, chaplain of St Christopher's Hospice, the Revd Julia French, the Revd Sacha Pearce and the Revd David Walford. A particular thanks goes to Dr Jeffrey Stephenson, my consultant in palliative care who kindly peer-reviewed the medical writing in the book. Thank you to Andrew Davison for inspiring this book and his continued guidance. My family have been an unwavering source of encouragement and love throughout and for them, I am forever grateful.

Andrew Davison: I would like to thank Caroline Russell Pung and Robin Griffith-Jones. They first encouraged me to volunteer at Sir Michael Sobell House in Oxford. I am profoundly grateful to have met, and worked with, many remarkable people there, both staff and patients. It was a crucial part of my path to ordained ministry. Students and staff at St Stephen's House, Wycliffe Hall and the Cambridge Theological Federation have talked to me about death and theology over the past seven years. Paul Butler provided an exemplary model – and instruction – for how to conduct a funeral. David Albert Jones and Tom Weinandy introduced me to Thomas Aquinas, and my debt to the great Dominican will be obvious. In the middle period of preparing this book, my grandmother was dying. The staff at North Ferriby Nursing Home, the local GP and members of my family demonstrated just how good care for the dying can be. My gratitude to them is profound because my gratitude to my grandmother, and my other grandparents, cannot properly be measured. *Requiescant in pace.*

Together we would like to express our gratitude to the Revd Andy Barton, the Revd Dr Michael Brierley, Helen Sims-Williams, the Revd James Hughesdon and Dr Jeffrey Stephenson for taking the time to both read through the manuscript and give us their invaluable feedback.

Foreword

In 1980, after four years in Chile and two in religious life, I returned to the practice of medicine, working as a junior doctor in the Plymouth cancer unit. There was, at that time, no local hospice and those patients we could not cure came back to us to die, often alone in a side ward. Most of them died without knowing that death was imminent because it was considered cruel to tell them the awful truth that they were dying.

In those first few months I was resident in the hospital and, finding the evenings lonely, I often spent time on the wards talking to the patients and the nurses. In particular, I spent time alone with the dying and little by little I learned that many patients, if not most, wanted to know what was happening to them and to talk about it.

One might have supposed that this was the chaplain's job, but as no one told them what was happening, and the patients' relatives forbade the doctors to tell the truth, the 'conspiracy of silence' reigned triumphant.

Things are very different now. The pioneers of the hospice movement learned on the job and they taught generations of doctors and nurses not only how to alleviate distressing symptoms, but how to be 'present' to dying patients and their families. Sioned Evans is a true daughter of the hospice movement. She and Andrew Davison write clearly and accurately of the experience of accompanying the dying. You can believe what they say.

Dr Sheila Cassidy

I

An Introduction to Palliative Care

This book is written jointly by a specialist in palliative care, who has spent time at a theological college, not as an ordinand but as an ordinand's spouse, where she also taught about death and dying, and a theologian with practical experience in this work. The acute need for such a book became apparent in the context of theological training, and this book is a response to that need.

Very few of those who enter ordained ministry have any experience of work with the dying. They feel at sea, perhaps even fearful, as they wonder how best they might serve. They do not know what they will say; they worry about making a situation worse and fear not being able to offer any real support.

Other books approach the pastoral and spiritual care of the dying from the perspective of the specialist, perhaps the hospice chaplain. We wanted to write a book that would offer practical help to those involved in ministry to the dying even if that is not the mainstay of their work, and to write it for lay Christians as well as clergy. This book looks at the principles lying behind the care that patients, and their loved ones, need. It seeks to allay fears by setting out what we might expect to encounter in such a context and discussing what we might say and do. Most important of all, it will put an emphasis on how to *be*.

The book presents the combination of their two author perspectives: thoughts from a palliative care doctor, who can offer guidance and reassurance, and from a theologian, who can talk about care of the dying from a context where it has been found for centuries, namely within the theological vision of the Church. It is our hope that our combined experience, of the holistic care of the dying and of Christian theology, will provide a useful and reassuring framework, and that you will find encouragement as you play your part in this vital ministry.

What is palliative care?

Before we discuss aspects of the care of the dying in detail, it is useful to take a step back and ask what we mean by palliative care in general. Various definitions have been given, but the 'gold standard' comes from the World Health Organization (WHO):

> Palliative care is an approach that improves the quality of life of patients and their families facing the problem associated with life-threatening illness, through the prevention and relief of suffering by means of early identification and impeccable assessment and treatment of pain and other problems, physical, psychosocial and spiritual. Palliative care:
> - provides relief from pain and other distressing symptoms;
> - affirms life and regards dying as a normal process;
> - intends neither to hasten or postpone death;
> - integrates the psychological and spiritual aspects of patient care;
> - offers a support system to help patients live as actively as possible until death;
> - offers a support system to help the family cope during the patient's illness and in their own bereavement;
> - uses a team approach to address the needs of patients and their families, including bereavement counselling, if indicated;
> - will enhance quality of life, and may also positively influence the course of illness;
> - is applicable early in the course of illness, in conjunction with other therapies that are intended to prolong life, such as chemotherapy or radiation therapy, and includes those investigations needed to better understand and manage distressing clinical complications.[1]

---

1 'WHO Definition of Palliative Care' <www.who.int/cancer/palliative/definition/en/>. The WHO definition of palliative care for children can be found in Chapter 11.

It is worth noting that this definition is not disease specific. Historically, the modern-day hospice movement was founded to care for patients dying from cancer. However, it was not long before the emphasis shifted, and patients with any progressive incurable disease were seen as needing, and worthy of, the same care. Today, patients being looked after under the palliative care umbrella include those with heart failure, respiratory failure (from chronic lung diseases) and progressive neurological diseases such as multiple sclerosis and motor neurone disease (more commonly referred to as amyotrophic lateral sclerosis or ALS in the USA). In different countries, the spectrum of diseases and causes of death will vary. Infectious diseases, for instance, cause a far greater proportion of deaths in the developing world than in the first world.

As the definition states, palliative care is not only about someone's final days, as someone approaches death (known as the terminal phase). It begins much earlier. Many patients are admitted to a hospice for control of their symptoms earlier on, and are soon discharged to their homes. The myth that there is 'only one way out' of the hospice is just that: a myth. Of course, many come to a hospice for their last days, or deteriorate after an otherwise more routine admission. All the same, much palliative care is focused on maintaining the best quality of *life*, however long that may be, and not simply on anticipating death. The principles of palliative care can be summed up in the words of Dame Cicely Saunders, founder of the modern hospice movement: 'You matter because you are you and you matter until the last moment of your life. We will do all we can not only to help you die peacefully but to live until you die.'[2]

The roots of hospice care go back into the depths of history, and to traditions of *hospitality* that, in Europe at least, have profoundly Christian roots. In its first usage, a 'hospice' was a guesthouse and the earliest hospitals (a word that derives from the same root in Latin as hospice) were places where the sick were given hospitality. Frequently, these early hospitals were attached

---

2 Cicely Saunders with introduction by David Clark, *Cicely Saunders: Selected Writings* – 1958–2004 (Oxford: Oxford University Press, 2006), p. xxiii.

to monasteries or other 'religious' houses. Orders of nuns, in particular, have played a remarkable role in the development of healthcare and in the very idea of the hospital and hospice. Taking the Church of England as an example, there is the Community of St John the Divine, whose work was dramatized in the BBC television series *Call the Midwife*, and the All Saints Sisters of the Poor, who founded the world's first children's hospice in 1982, in Oxford.

Hospitals in many countries often have religious roots, even if today they are run by civic government. Within public hospitals, from the nineteenth century onwards, care of the dying (or 'incurables') began to receive more attention. An important step was the foundation of Our Lady's Hospice in Dublin by the Irish Sisters of Charity in the late nineteenth century. This marks a newly acute focus on the dying as a distinct group, needing a particular sort of care. This hospice was followed by another, St Joseph's, founded by the same order in London 16 years later.[3]

The growth of the palliative care movement: Dame Cicely Saunders

The pioneer of the modern hospice movement was Dame Cicely Saunders (1919–2005). We can get close to much that lies at the heart of Christian care of the dying through attention to the example set by this woman. She responded zealously, and patiently, to a call that was to change the face of medical care.

After leaving school, Cicely gained a place at Oxford University to study politics, philosophy and economics. At the end of her first year, the Second World War broke out. She began to feel uneasy about studying while the country was at war, and as a result she left Oxford to train as a nurse at St Thomas' Hospital in London. Her nursing career was curtailed by a back problem, but during that time she came to love being with patients – a disposition that was to lie behind all that she went on to achieve. The next step

---

3 Shirley du Boulay and Marianne Rankin, *Cicely Saunders: The Founder of the Modern Hospice Movement* (London: SPCK, 2007), p. 185.

of that journey was to train as an 'almoner': known today as a medical social worker.[4]

The watershed moment for Saunders came with her Christian conversion in 1945, after which she became a member of the evangelical congregation at All Souls', Langham Place in London. John Stott became its curate in the year of her conversion and was to become a profound influence in her work. Her new love for God demanded a practical response and she asked, 'What have I got to do to say thank you and serve?'[5] The answer came in the unexpected form of a relationship with a patient, David Tasma, in 1948. He was a 40-year-old Polish Jew from the Warsaw ghetto who called himself an agnostic. He was dying from cancer in a busy London hospital. Cicely Saunders was his almoner.

What started as a professional relationship led to deep love and affection. Their conversations revolved around his unfulfilled life, his physical pain and his loneliness. Together they spoke about what could be done for him and for others in his situation. Tasma brought into sharp focus the desperate need at that time, in the United Kingdom and beyond, for better care for dying people. Cicely's particular gift was to recognize that dying people experience not only physical pain, but emotional, social and spiritual pain too. This combination she named 'total pain'.[6] Her response was to propose holistic care (from the Greek word *holos*, meaning whole or entire). She wanted to create a place where dying people would receive care for every dimension of their need. In his will, David Tasma left Cicely £500. With permission from the hospital, she took the money and used it to begin to realize her dream. Her experience with Tasma, as much as this capital sum, laid the foundations of her vision.

Following Tasma's death, Cicely knew that she wanted to work with the dying, but still needed to test her call. She made contact with St Luke's, one of the places in London that already cared

---

4 The details of her life are taken from du Boulay and Rankin, *Cicely Saunders*, as is material in the discussion of the later hospice movement.

5 Du Boulay and Rankin, *Cicely Saunders*, p. 32.

6 Caroline Richmond, 'Obituary: Dame Cicely Saunders', *British Medical Journal*, 331 (2005), p. 238.

for the dying. She became a volunteer there and remained so for seven years. St Luke's had been founded in 1893 by Dr Howard Barrett, at the time Medical Director of the West London Mission, a Wesleyan initiative, working alongside his brother-in-law, the Revd Hugh Price Hughes, their Chief Missioner. St Luke's was originally known as 'A Home for the Dying Poor'.[7] His desire was to give the dying poor a 'place of peace', instead of the squalid conditions where they might otherwise die. This made him the first doctor to set up an institution for patients with incurable diseases. By the time Cicely Saunders volunteered there, it had grown significantly.[8]

What Cicely observed and learned at St Luke's came to underpin the modern hospice movement. In the words of her biography:

> It was a home rather than a hospital, it was free – patients only contributing if they had the means and wished to do so; it had a strong religious basis and yet was interdenominational; most crucially of all, the staff were intensely interested in the patients as individuals.[9]

It had a distinctive ethos:

> Although all patients are alike in that they are 'dying', each has his [sic] own separate life and it is the duty of the visiting sister to regard with absolute sanctity the individuality of each one and to try and reach that which makes the man *himself* and does not belong to another.[10]

That ethos, laid down in 1905, holds today throughout palliative care.

Cicely wanted to make this care available to many, not just a few. She took this task as the answer to her prayer concerning

---

7 Du Boulay and Rankin, *Cicely Saunders*, p. 38.

8 Grace Goldin, 'A Protohospice at the Turn of the Century, St. Luke's House, London, 1893–1921', *Journal of the History of Medicine and Allied Sciences*, 36 (1981), pp. 383–415.

9 Du Boulay and Rankin, *Cicely Saunders*, pp. 38–9.

10 Du Boulay and Rankin, *Cicely Saunders*, p. 39.

how to serve God. She was to pioneer a new field of medicine, one that would embrace the dying patient and counter the then current thinking that 'there is nothing more we can do'. Her legacy is that these principles have entered mainstream medicine.

At first, however, there were sizeable obstacles. Cicely was told that she would not make a real difference unless she trained as a doctor. She therefore returned to St Thomas', this time for medical training, qualifying in 1957, at the then remarkably advanced age of 39. After completing junior medical posts, she was given a significant break: a research scholarship at St Mary's Hospital, London, to look at pain in the terminally ill. Until then, this subject had been scandalously neglected.

Cicely carried out much of her research at St Joseph's Hospice in Hackney, in London's East End. In the 1950s it had around 150 beds, with about a third dedicated to the care of the terminally ill. There were a few trained nurses on the staff from the Irish Sisters, and the remainder were auxiliaries. Although immensely caring, the nurses had no specific training in responding to the particular needs of the dying. Neither was there a resident doctor: just two local GPs who could be called upon. Thus it was that Cicely Saunders found herself as the first doctor to specialize in the care of the dying. From that base, she established that a regular dosage of painkillers enabled patients to face the emotional and spiritual components of their suffering.

On 24 June 1959 Cicely read these words from Psalm 37: 'Commit thy way unto the Lord; trust also in Him; and He shall bring it to pass.' She took this as a 'tap on the shoulder; it was time for her to act'.[11] After a period on retreat she returned to work to set up St Christopher's Hospice, which eventually opened in July 1967.

Money had to be raised, building plans agreed and a devoted pioneering team created in order to achieve the vision. Cicely wanted the hospice to be both a medical and a Christian foundation and was keen to maintain those roots as the hospice grew. Before the foundations were laid, the Bishop of Stepney, Evered

---

11 Du Boulay and Rankin, *Cicely Saunders*, p. 60.

Lunt, summed up the aim of the hospice: 'So to minister to the whole personality that those whom we shall serve may be able to lose their fear of death and to find in it, not primarily an end of life in this world but the beginning of a fuller life in the world to come.'[12] The architecture reflected this vision, with the chapel positioned in the centre, but there was nothing sectarian about this vision: Cicely saw a strong Christian foundation as perfectly able to welcome those of all faiths and none, and there was ecumenical involvement in the dedication of the chapel. The name St Christopher was chosen as being the patron saint of travellers; here was a place where people would come to travel the last part of their journey.

Almost immediately, St Christopher's became an internationally renowned centre for medical learning and research. That reputation remains to this day. Lunt recognized another enduring insight about the care of the dying when he wrote that here the 'Church and medical professions together will make provisions in all aspects' not only for the patient but also 'for the care of the family'.[13] Generations of clergy-in-training and medical students alike have had placements at St Christopher's, gaining valuable experience for the benefit of other communities.

The work that Cicely Saunders began in London has influenced the care of the dying throughout the world. She spent much of her time promoting the modern hospice movement in a whirlwind of speaking engagements both across the United Kingdom and abroad. The USA and Canada were among the first to follow her lead, with their own pioneers, and many medics from these countries visited St Christopher's.

During the 1970s, four models of palliative care developed, all influenced in one way or another by St Christopher's.[14] The first is the stand-alone hospice, like St Christopher's itself. In the UK, these followed in Sheffield, Manchester and Worthing. In 1976, Sir Michael Sobell House Hospice was opened in Oxford. Dr

---

12 Du Boulay and Rankin, *Cicely Saunders*, p. 125.

13 The Bishop of Stepney, St Christopher's Day Meeting, 28 November 1964. Quoted in du Boulay and Rankin, *Cicely Saunders*, p. 119.

14 Du Boulay and Rankin, *Cicely Saunders*, p. 186.

Robert Twycross, another pioneer, was their first medical director and served there until 2001. By the 1980s, there were some 73 such hospices in the UK.

At this time, Professor Eric Wilkes, a fellow pioneer in palliative care, began promoting the need for an integrated system of care that would allow for the dissemination of teaching and care across general practice, hospitals and hospices. From this, the other three models emerged. The first is the palliative care unit, situated on a hospital campus, with Sir Michael Sobell House in Oxford being an early example. Second is home care, where a team of professionals look after the dying in their own homes. This model began at St Christopher's in 1969 and reached the USA five years later. Third, there are hospital support teams. The first such team was started in St Luke's Hospital, New York, by Carlton Sweetser, who had spent a sabbatical at St Christopher's. A similar team began operating at St Thomas' Hospital in London in 1977. The current model for palliative care services incorporates all of these models. In 1987, the Royal College of Physicians recognized Palliative Medicine as a speciality in its own right: the discipline's watershed.

Palliative care today

The palliative care service you are likely to encounter today will almost certainly be fully integrated. That is to say, local palliative care services will work together to provide co-ordinated care to patients at home, in hospital and in a hospice. Home care is also available to nursing and residential homes in an advisory capacity. The principal benefit here comes in communication between different teams and from a multi-dimensional perspective on deciding how best to serve the patient's needs. It is an excellent way to ensure that the patient remains central. Day-care services are also located at many hospices, providing a welcome break for both patients and families.

Most palliative care services will offer a variety of expertise within their team. Alongside doctors, nurses, healthcare assistants

(or auxiliary nurses) and chaplains, we might find physio-
therapists, occupational therapists, social workers, pharmacists,
complementary therapists, art and music therapists, psychologists
and counsellors.

Hospices are usually run as charities. Most of their funding comes from charitable giving and fundraising, with a small
proportion from the government. Hospices rely to an enormous
extent on the support of volunteers, who undertake a variety of
essential roles such as serving meals, working on reception, and
driving patients to and from hospice day care.

A priest, minister or other visitor will be among the members
of this team, whether the setting is in the home, hospital, hospice
or nursing home. By and large, patients will be asked about their
religious beliefs on admission, or more generic questions are
explored concerning spirituality. This provides an opportunity for
the patient to identify himself as a Christian and specify his wishes
for Christian pastoral and sacramental care. A note is usually
made of whether the patient is a member of a congregation, and
of the name of the priest or minister.

Visiting ministers are made welcome and the note of familiarity
that they bring can be a great support to the patient. The hospice
chaplain will usually liaise with the parish or local minister about
the spiritual support that will be provided.

Our privilege and the plight of others

One of the tragedies in current world healthcare is the lack of
provision of palliative care in the developing world. The need
is great: Help the Hospices estimates that 100 million people
worldwide, including patients and carers, would benefit from
palliative care. Unfortunately, only a small minority have access
to the care from which they could so much benefit. For example,
in India it is believed that fewer than 1 per cent of those who
need palliative care can access it. Many people die in pain,
without adequate support for themselves and their families.

The barriers are complex and varied. The concept of palliative care itself is unknown in some countries, and a variety of presuppositions that can mitigate against the best care at the end of life (sometimes similar to those in the West, and sometimes different) remain to be addressed. In particular, many doctors fear morphine, considering it to be a dangerous drug, and avoid using it. Its association with death is an added barrier. Appropriately used, however, morphine is often a central plank in pain relief. It is relatively cheap to produce, but cost remains a factor in some countries.

The pioneering work that has been and is being carried out in many developing countries where palliative care is a scarce resource should serve to inspire us both to contribute to that endeavour and to be grateful for what we have nearer to home. Notable contributions have been made by Dr Anne Merriman in Uganda, and by Dr Cynthia Goh and Dr Rosalie Shaw within the Asia Pacific Palliative Care Network (APHN).

Organizations such as Help the Hospices and the International Association of Palliative Care are working hard to co-operate with medics and others in developing countries, to provide education and training, and also to facilitate a discussion as to what form indigenization of palliative care would take in different countries. This work is important, but change is needed at the level of global policy. Christian churches and organizations play an important role in this effort to bring basic palliative care to the majority who still lack it.

Back to Dame Cicely

Cicely Saunders received personal recognition for her phenomenal achievements, including fellowships from various Royal Colleges, the Templeton Prize for outstanding efforts in the field of religion, a Damehood, the Order of Merit (the highest honour within the British system), and a rare doctorate in medicine conferred directly by the Archbishop of Canterbury.

She died in 2005 at St Christopher's Hospice. It was fitting that she received care in the place she had founded. She had been suffering from breast cancer since 2002. She was said to be very happy with the care that she received, reaping the fruits of her labour first-hand. A memorial service at Westminster Abbey was attended by almost 2,000 people.[15]

15 Few figures from the twentieth century so obviously deserve to be added in the calendar of the Church of England.

2

Death in Christian Theology

Christian theologians approach death from the perspective of life. We do this for two reasons. One is a matter of humility. Human beings can only approach death from our perspective: the perspective of those who are living before death. Of death itself, we know little. The other reason that we look at death through the lens of life is that we understand Christ to have overcome death. Ultimately, therefore, life, and not death, has the final word.

Of death itself, as we have said, we know little. As Shakespeare's Hamlet puts it, death is 'the undiscover'd country from whose bourn / No traveller returns'. In a sense, however, Hamlet was wrong. One traveller has passed through death, and returned (if we lay no emphasis on Lazarus and others raised to life in the Gospels, and elsewhere): Jesus Christ. Because of his rising again, we can say with the Nicene Creed that 'We look for the resurrection of the dead, and the life of the world to come.'[1]

Death is a theological subject. The populace at large recognize that. In the face of death, many people turn to the local church. This places a heavy responsibility upon clergy, in particular, in that they are treated as experts on death, but who can or would claim such expertise? Responding to questions about the nature of death calls for a combination of humility and confidence: humility in face of the 'undiscover'd' element, and a simple confidence because of the death and resurrection of Christ. In contrast, a know-it-all expert on the 'theology of death' is not likely to be the

---

1 Translation from *Common Worship: Services and Prayers for the Church of England* (London: Church House Publishing, 2000).

right person to work with the dying, take a funeral, or comfort the bereaved. Our task is both to bear witness to the faith of the Church and not to exceed the Church in her reticence.

At the heart of our message is the news that, in Jesus, God is no stranger to death. Perhaps nothing in the whole tradition bears a more remarkable witness to this than a single word, 'buried', in the Creed: 'he was crucified, died and was *buried*'.[2] Jesus himself shared our human life all the way to death, and beyond death, to burial.

We do not even need to read to the end of the Gospels to find this identification. From the very beginning, Christ and his family were no strangers to death and grief. We are only two chapters into Matthew's Gospel when we come upon the massacre of the Holy Innocents, or two chapters into Luke when we read Simeon's words to Mary that 'a sword will pierce your own soul too'.[3] When Jesus tarried in the temple, his parents suffered loss.[4] This is a prefiguration of his death and, like his death, it was over-come on the third day. Moreover, just as Christ was 'a man of sorrows, and acquainted with grief',[5] so were the early Christians. In Rome, for instance, we can visit the catacombs and see their tombs, some the resting place of martyrs, stretching on and on.

In the finding in the temple, we recognize something about the heart of grief: grief is about loss. Conversely, loss of every kind has been called an anticipation of death.[6] In his poem 'Spring and Fall: To a Young Child', Gerard Manley Hopkins went so

---

2 Karl Barth makes something of this in his commentary on the Apostles' Creed, *Credo* (London: Hodder & Stoughton, 1936), translated by J. Strathearn McNab, pp. 84–7.

3 Matt. 2.16–18; Luke 2.35.

4 Luke 2.42–51.

5 Isa. 53.3 (KSV) It may be worth remembering, when we come across some-one who is dealing with disfigurement through illness, that Christ also shared in *this*. The Christian tradition read in the book of Isaiah a prophecy of the result of flogging and crucifixion: 'so marred was his appearance, beyond human sem-blance, and his form beyond that of mortals' (Isa. 52.14).

6 From Elizabeth Bishop (1911–79) we have a poem ('One Art') about mastering the art of losing things, seen as just such an anticipation of death.

far as to propose that in every loss we grieve our own death in advance. This surely goes too far, but it is an eloquent witness to the connection. Death is a loss for those who are left behind; death is perhaps also loss for the one who dies, and the sum of all losses, as C. S. Lewis suggested.[7]

What is death?

We use the word 'death' in English in two ways. It names an event and a state: it describes both 'dying' and 'being dead'. When we talk about death, it is worth bearing in mind which sense we mean. From a theological perspective, the two senses are related: one is the boundary of the other. For the materialist, on the other hand, only the first sense is meaningful ('dying'). The materialist, who thinks that there is *only matter*, cannot talk about 'being dead'. However, since the Christian believes that human beings are both material and more than material, 'being dead' can make sense. This is reflected in the ways in which death is described, for instance as the moment when 'the soul departs from the body'. As long as we are careful what we mean by 'soul' – and we return to this subject below – this is not such a bad definition of death. Our word 'animated' comes from *anima*, the Latin word for the soul. Death is when the body is no longer animated, so as to constitute a living person.

From a biological point of view, the event of death can be quite difficult to define. Death involves the cessation of the co-ordinated processes of the body, processes that are their own sort of animation or movement. Those processes, however, may not all cease at precisely the same time. The more complicated ('higher') functions of the brain may cease before the heart stops beating. For obvious reasons, the processes of the brain, heart and lungs are particularly significant when it comes to defining death. While we will not dwell on these biological questions here, they are important when it comes to some questions of medical ethics,

---

7 *A Grief Observed* (London: Faber and Faber, 1961), p. 41.

such as when it is morally acceptable to switch off a life-support machine, or remove organs for transplantation.[8]

Christian theology uses the language of death to talk about more than physical death. We talk of sin, for instance, as a kind of death. This not necessarily elliptical or 'metaphorical' usage. The state of 'spiritual death', of rebellion against God, may be the primary meaning of death.[9] Biblical authors talk about sin and death in the same breath, because sin is a separation from God. Death and sin are each an estrangement or sundering. In this life, and beyond, God works to undo the estrangement of sin, such that we can ultimately share in Christ's victory over physical death. There may be comfort here. Viewed from eternity, although we all have to die, physical death approached in union with God is less to be dreaded than life lived without him.

Death and the atonement

Christian theologians talk about redemption using the word 'atonement'. It comes from an early English root pointing to the overcoming of separation. Atonement is literally at-one-ment. Atonement is that work of God by which we are restored to fellowship with him, and with one another, and he heals the wounds caused by sin.

The work of atonement cannot be entirely fathomed, however many words we use. The Bible bears witness to this, since it contains a multitude of images for redemption. This suggests that we need many angles on salvation in order to appreciate even some of what God has done for us. One way or another, many of these images relate to death.

One popular description of salvation in the Early Church was that Christ redeemed us as a *victor*. There is much of this in the

8 These questions have recently been discussed in a powerful book by the physician and medical ethicist Jeffrey Bishop entitled *The Anticipatory Corpse: Medicine, Power, and the Care of the Dying* (Notre Dame, IN: University of Notre Dame Press, 2011).

9 We talk about 'mortal' sin (for instance, in 1 John 5.16–17) as the sort of sin that destroys our relationship with God.

New Testament, for instance in the various showdowns between Jesus and the powers of evil, or sickness. We find it in interpretations of the crucifixion as a 'triumph' over the rulers of this world (usually taken to be demonic powers), as in Colossians 2.15. The link to death is made clear there, as it is in Hebrews:

> Since, therefore, the children share flesh and blood, he [Jesus] himself likewise shared the same things, so that through death he might destroy the one who has the power of death, that is, the devil, and free those who all their lives were held in slavery by the fear of death. (Heb. 2.14–15)

The liturgical tradition of the Church has taken up this theme joyfully. In the Orthodox Churches, the 'Easter Proclamation' is sung repeatedly on Easter Day: 'Christ is risen from the dead, trampling down death by death, and on those in the tombs bestowing life!' Similar ideas are expressed in the Western Church's 'Easter Sequence' and in Martin Luther's chorale *Christ lag in Todes Banden* ('Christ lay in death's bonds'):

> Jesus Christ, God's son,
> has come in our place,
> and has done away with sin,
> thereby taking from death
> all his rights and power,
> nothing remains but death's form;
> he has lost his sting.
> Hallelujah!
>
> It was a strange battle,
> that death and life waged,
> life claimed the victory,
> it devoured death.
> The scripture had prophesied this,
> how one death gobbled up the other,
> a mockery has been made out of death.
> Hallelujah![10]

---

10 Verses 3 and 4. Translation © Pamela Dellal.

This way of talking about Christ's death, as a battle with death personified, does not say every last thing we want to say about redemption, but it has been an important part of the Christian interpretation of the cross and resurrection, and it can be helpful. Another prominent account of the atonement is in terms of *substitution*. Today that is often cast in terms of Christ bearing the punishment, in death, that was due to the human race. In earlier times, the emphasis was often subtly, but significantly, different. Anselm of Canterbury wrote that Christ offered a debt of honour to God, whom we had offended by our sin, in a way that we could not put right.[11] Thomas Aquinas argued much the same: Christ offered love to the Father on our behalf, giving 'more to God than was required to compensate for the offence of the whole human race'.[12] Approached this way, Christ is our substitute, not in the sense that God punished him *instead of us*, but rather in that Christ did something *for us*, which we could not do, and as a consequence, God punishes neither him nor us.

Substitution has an important place in accounts of the atonement. Whatever else Christians have also wanted to say about the death of Christ, there has usually been some sense of him taking our place. All the same, substitution only really works on the basis of solidarity, for all that those two ideas are sometimes seen as opposites. Turning back to Hebrews, we read that Christ came so that 'by the grace of God he might taste death for everyone' (Heb. 2.9). There are elements of exchange, representation and substitution here. At the same time, the author makes it clear that this can only happen on the basis of solidarity: the Son of God became one of us. Christ did not simply die *instead* of us but rather *with* us, and one because of the other. From the earliest days of the Church, we find writers, and preachers, saying that God redeems us by being with us. Whatever God touches can come back to life, and in Christ God embraces all of what it means to be human, filling it with his life. In Christ, God even shares our death, so that his healing and life-giving touch may be felt there as well.

---

11 In *Cur Deus Homo*.
12 *Summa Theologiae* III.48.2. See also III.49.4.

If we only emphasize the 'instead of us', our position can seem rather cold: we are redeemed, but not everyone is comforted by matters of fact. Putting emphasis on the 'with us' dimension can be pastorally very helpful.

The final angle on the atonement to be considered is that of example. By itself, this is far from enough: Christ's redemption changed the state of the world; it did not simply change our ideas. Christ died to rescue us, not simply to urge us on to strive a little harder and sort ourselves out. All the same, without this model, of Christ as our example, we do miss something. Whatever substitution means, it does not mean that Christ died so that we do not have to. Bar the Second Coming, we *will* all die. Christ did not die to prevent us from dying; Christ died so that our death could be different. He taught us what to die for and, following his example, many have indeed given their lives for God, love and justice. As Stanley Hauerwas put it, 'Dying is not the tragedy'; rather, from the Christian point of view, the truest tragedy is 'dying for the wrong thing'.[13]

Christ not only showed us what to be prepared to die for, he showed us how to die. The ethicist Michael Banner has pointed out that Christ provided an ideal pattern for the Christian when it comes to preparation for death in the Seven Last Words (or Sayings) from the cross.[14]

The first 'word' picks up on the theme of forgiving others: 'Father, forgive them; for they do not know what they are doing' (Luke 23.34). The importance of forgiveness is present, right at the start. We discuss forgiveness in Chapters 4 and 8. The next word underlines the assurance of forgiveness and salvation for all who turn to Christ: 'Truly I tell you, today you will be with me in Paradise' (Luke 23.43). The words of Jesus to Mary and John, which traditionally follow, remind us of the importance of attending to practical matters: 'Woman, here is your son ... Here is your mother.' We read that 'from that hour the disciple took

13 'Memory, Community, and the Reasons for Living: Reflections: Suicide and Euthanasia', in *The Hauerwas Reader* (Durham, NC: Duke University Press, 2001), pp. 577–95, p. 587.
14 'Thought for the Day', BBC Radio Four, 28 April 2013.

her into his own home' (John 19.26–27). In the fourth word, we encounter the desolation of Christ: 'Eli, Eli, lema sabachthani? [that is] My God, my God, why have you forsaken me?' (Matt. 27.46). These may be the most devastating words ever uttered, and they remind us that Christ has shared with us in even our utmost desolation. The next word underlines everything that we say in subsequent chapters about the importance of good medical care and concern for all of a patient's needs. In death, Christ too experienced bodily need: 'I am thirsty' (John 19.28). Such needs are to be met, as much as we are able. The penultimate word illustrates the very heart of Christian dying, that ultimately we can do no more, and need do no more, than commend ourselves to God our Father: 'Father, into your hands I commend my spirit' (Luke 23.46). Finally, we have Christ's assurance, not simply that his earthly life had reached its end, but that our salvation has been accomplished: 'It is finished' (John 19.30).

Death as enemy and friend

We probably all know situations when someone has lost a relative and has been told by a well-meaning Christian friend that there is 'no need to be sad', since this person, perhaps a mother or father, 'is now with Jesus'. The loved one is with Jesus, so – the implication goes – what's the problem?

In Chapter 6, on communication, we suggest that *being with* someone may be the best we can offer in these circumstances, and that words – especially words that may appear glib – are not necessarily the most appropriate response. Certainly, few people who are grieving will find it quite so easy to situate their loss within the comfort of an eternal perspective. It may not even be right to do so too easily. Yes, in one sense, all is well: he or she now sees Jesus, just as St Paul wrote that he wished 'to depart and be with Christ' (Phil. 1.23). On the other hand, the Bible also clearly treats death as a problem.

Christian theology, in short, sees death in both a negative and a positive light; it is both a good and an ill. Different traditions of faith and piety will place the emphasis in a different place on this continuum. Both faith and piety can be enriched if we keep hold of both elements.

On the one hand, death is 'the last enemy' (1 Cor. 15.26). This angle was revived in the twentieth century by Gustaf Aulén, who placed a renewed emphasis on the redemption-as-victory model of the atonement, as discussed above. In the thirteenth century, Thomas Aquinas stressed that death is our enemy and that it is therefore possible 'for someone to fear death too little'.[15]

On the other hand, there is that desire of Paul's 'to depart and be with Christ, for that is far better'. One of Johann Sebastian Bach's most beautiful works is a setting of a German hymn written in this vein:

Come, sweet death, come blessed rest!
Come lead me to peace
For I am weary of the world,
Oh come! I wait for you,
Come soon and lead me,
Close my eyes.
Come, blessed rest![16]

The ambiguity of the relation between death-as-loss and death-as-gain is related in another passage from Paul: do not 'grieve as others do who have no hope', he wrote to the Thessalonians (1 Thess. 4.13). He was not telling them to avoid grieving altogether, just not to grieve as those without hope. Jesus said 'blessed are those who mourn' (Matt. 5.4) and elsewhere Paul tells us to 'weep with those who weep' (Rom. 12.15).

For another sense of the variety of the Christian tradition on this point, we have only to turn to two close friends and colleagues among the Fathers of the Church: St Ambrose (c. AD 330–397) and St Augustine (AD 354–430). We rarely find direct contradiction between the Fathers, and least of all between Augustine

---

15 *Summa Theologiae* II-II.126.1.
16 *Komm, süßer Tod, komm selge Ruh!* Translator unknown.

and his teacher. All the same, taking their thought as a whole, Ambrose tended to see death as a good thing, which can be made bad, whereas for Augustine death is a bad thing, which can be made good.[17]

Pope Benedict XVI mentioned Ambrose's position in his encyclical *Spe Salvi*, quoting a funeral oration of Ambrose: life would be unbearable without death, he wrote; it would be interminable. In any case, thought Ambrose, life is often pretty awful already. In contrast, Augustine stressed that Paul presents death in the language of punishment (as does the author of Genesis). In any case, thought Augustine, death stands as an evil in relation to the innate human will to self-preservation. This sense that death is an evil that we suffer was underlined by the early Christians when they insisted that martyrdom should not be sought out for its own sake: life is good and not to be thrown away. These ideas also undergird the Christian prohibition on suicide.[18]

Death is not the only topic on which Christian theology presents more than one view, where the Church gives us a more than one-dimensional vision. We have several models for the atonement, for instance, and different approaches to the doctrine of the Trinity, which variously either stress the one (while upholding the three) or the three (while upholding the one). This variety is a good thing. From the breadth of the theological tradition, the preacher and pastor can garner resources for teaching and pastoral care: 'Therefore every scribe who has been trained for the kingdom of heaven', said Christ, 'is like the master of a household who brings out of his treasure what is new and what is old' (Matt. 13.52).

---

17 See David Albert Jones, *Approaching the End: A Theological Exploration of Death and Dying* (Oxford: Oxford University Press, 2007): pp. 24–6 on Ambrose and pp. 37–55 on Augustine. Jones's book is highly recommended.

18 A theological note of pastoral compassion is not out of place here. If we see life as a supreme good, then anyone who neglects or hates his or her own life must be in an extreme state of mental anguish or misunderstanding. This could be said, at least in many cases, to mitigate against treating suicide as a mortal sin. The very point that the human being has an innate and rational will to self-preservation, which is what makes suicide a sin, also renders suicide supremely 'irrational', thereby lessening culpability.

Making use of that treasure calls for prudence. When it comes to death, the tradition provides resources for sympathy with a young person who laments the prospect of death; it also provides resources for sympathy with the person, worn out by illness, who seeks a departure. We can commiserate and encourage, but our commiseration should not, and need not, be glib. Sometimes a grieving family will not want easy comfort. They may find more consolation in the judgement of the Church that death is indeed 'the ultimate and most terrible evil of this life',[19] to quote Aquinas again, than in being told that death is but a journey to another room.[20]

The positive-and-negative tension can also be approached in terms of the virtue of hope. In face of death, we seek for hope. Hope is a virtue and, like other virtues, it is opposed not to one vice but to two. Hope lies between despair and presumption: despair, which is supposing that God cannot save us, and presumption, which supposes that we do not need saving. We can all vary over how we approach death in general, and any particular death, but we might pray not to fall into these two extremes: despair or presumption.

The soul

Much of what we say about death is expressed in terms of the body, the soul and their relation.[21] Here we again find two extremes to avoid. One is materialism: the notion that there is nothing to a

---

19 *Summa Theologiae* II-II.64.4.

20 This line comes from Henry Scott Holland's sermon on death of 1910, 'The King of Terrors'. The immediate passage from which it comes is popular at funerals. It begins 'Death is nothing at all. It does not count. I have only slipped away into the next room. Nothing has happened. Everything remains exactly as it was.' This is not a position that Scott Holland was endorsing, however. The sermon lays out two views of death, as we are in this chapter, and this optimistic view could not last, he thought. Eventually we lament the loss and realize that 'death is, after all, a fearful thing'.

21 The soul is discussed at greater length in Andrew Davison, *The Love of Wisdom: An Introduction to Philosophy for Theologians* (London: SCM Press, 2013).

human being but her atoms. On a rigorously materialist account, no talk of the soul, the person or even the mind can be justified. Viewed from this perspective, it can be difficult to see quite what death means at all. The 'person' was never really 'alive' in the first place, not in the way we usually mean 'person' or 'alive'.

It is easy to see why Christians have rejected this position. More beguiling, but problematic all the same, has been the dualist tradition stemming from Plato. The soul and the body, on this view, are basically independent, despite being entwined in this life. For the dualist, personhood resides in the soul: I *am* my soul; I merely *have* a body. Plato went so far as to call the body the 'prison' of the soul.[22] This position was taken to its logical conclusion by a group of early Christian heretics called Gnostics. They talked about salvation as freedom from the body, and from materiality in general. Matter, they thought, was the creation of an evil god. In reply, the Church stressed that matter is a good part of God's good creation.

The Fathers of the Church saw that the Gnostics had got it wrong. That did not stop traditions of theology and spirituality from following Plato – often a helpful figure – in an unhelpful direction when it comes to the soul. The language of *having* a body rather than *being* a body persisted, for instance. That is not to say that more satisfactory formulations were not sometimes put forward. St Maximus the Confessor (580–662), for instance, wrote: 'It is inconceivable to speak of the soul and the body except in relation to each other ... The relation between them is immutable.'[23] Some of the thinking that kept the Church on the right track over this question revolved around death and the care of the dead body. Christians did not treat the body as a discarded husk; they treated it as integral to who the person was, is and one day will be again. Maximus wrote that after death, the soul is still 'the soul of a human being, indeed the soul of a certain human

---

22 *Phaedo*, 62b.

23 *Ambiguum* 6, §1101. Translation from Paul Blowers and Robert Louis Wilken, *On the Cosmic Mystery of Jesus Christ: Selected Writings from St Maximus* (New York, St Vladimir's Seminary Press, 2003), p. 74.

being'. That means that 'the body, after its separation from the soul,' is not a body in general but 'the body of a certain man [or woman], even though it will ... be broken down into the elements from which it was composed'.[24]

The breakthrough for knowing how to express all of this well came in the thirteenth century, with the rediscovery of Aristotle. It turned out that, with a little tweaking, Aristotle could help Christian theologians to say just what they wanted to say. Aristotle's idea – and we explore this terminology below – was that 'the soul is the form of the body'.

Unpacking this calls for a paragraph or two of light philosophy. The basic observation is that any physical thing is both material and also more than just a pile of so much matter. Aristotle's angle on this was to say that every physical thing has two aspects: what it is *made from* and what it *is*; its stuff and what that stuff adds up to. The stuff he called 'matter' and what the stuff amounts to he called 'form'. This is not to say that form and matter are two different 'things'. There is one *thing* but we can usefully look at it from two perspectives: the material perspective and the formal perspective. We might take the example of a cup. The form is what the cup is; the matter is what it is made from. The form is what is special and unique about the cup; the matter is what is not unique (clay, ultimately atoms, and beyond that simply being-material-as-such). The matter happens to be the matter of a cup, but it could be the matter of something else.

Turning back to the soul, our proposal is that 'the soul is the form of the body'. What the cup-ishness of the cup is to the cup, so my soul is to me. When I talk about my soul, I talk about *me*: a 'me' that is not separate from my body, but is what my body means and amounts to. This is not unscientific. After all, how any part of me behaves only makes full sense in terms of its connection to some sort of whole: the whole that is me.

Saying that the soul is the form of the body means that body and soul are tightly interwoven: as tightly interwoven as can be imagined. My soul is not a separate part of me, any more than

---

24 *Ambiguum* 7, §1101.

the cup-ishness of the cup can be separated from the cup. It is just that I can explain myself from the perspective of matter, and in that way I describe my body, or I can explain myself from the perspective of what that body adds up to, and in that way I describe my soul. Notice how different, and helpfully earthy, this is in comparison to the idea that my soul is something added to my body.

The difference between the form of a cup and a soul is that souls are the forms of living things. As we saw above, the Latin word for soul is *anima* and a soul is the form of an *animated* thing: of something with an inner movement. On this basis, Aristotle would say that plants and animals also have 'souls', in that they add up to something that moves. The difference is that human beings are rational: they have rational souls.

If I drop a cup on a hard floor, it smashes. The stuff is the same; the matter has not changed. The cup has been destroyed, however. The matter no longer has the form of a cup. It now has the form of shards of pottery. When something is broken, or dies, its form passes and a new form arrives.

That brings us to the part of Aristotle's scheme that Christians have wanted to change. According to the Christian vision of things, God is particularly interested in each human being as an individual (although he is also interested in human communities). God creates a human being to be different from other things, even from other animals: he creates human forms, or souls, to be immortal. For some theologians, that means that human souls are immortal from their first moment of existence. We could, however, look at this from the other end of human life. Maybe the human soul is more like that form of a cup, for instance, which perishes when it is broken. The difference would then be that God will not let the human soul perish at death. God intervenes to preserve our self or identity, form or soul, at that moment. The body dies but its form is held in God's hand. Immortality, on that view, is a gift given at the end rather than a gift given at the beginning.

Psalm 121 is a favourite psalm at funerals. It ends 'The LORD shall preserve thee from all evil; yea, it is even he that shall keep thy soul. The LORD shall preserve thy going out, and thy coming in, from this time forth for evermore.'[25] When we die – a time of 'going out' from this world and of 'coming in' to God's presence – the Lord preserves us from the evil of dissolution and 'keeps thy soul'. We know ourselves to be fragile, but at death we find that 'The eternal God is thy refuge, and underneath are the everlasting arms' (Deut. 33.27 AV).[26]

With the idea of the soul in place we can bring together some significant topics from this chapter. First, 'What is death?' Death is that moment when the soul – or life or person – to whose tune the processes of the body have previously danced, is no longer there. After death, the matter of this particular body no longer adds up to being that particular person, as it once did. The soul is gone. Death is not, however, total and abject loss. God preserves the essence of the person, the soul – again, what that body added up to – in his mercy. This gives us an angle on a second question: 'Is death friend or foe?' In part, it is an evil, since it involves the separation of *who* we are, our soul, from *how* we should be, which is bodily. Yet death is not an unmitigated evil, since that 'who we are' is preserved, even taken to God. Third, this account also stresses that the end of the Christian story in general has to be the resurrection of the body, as it was for Christ in particular. A soul is the form of a body, so God will not leave the story of salvation with disembodied souls. Salvation ultimately restores our souls to be what they ought to be, and properly are, namely the form of a (now glorified) body. As the Apostles' Creed ends. 'I believe in … the resurrection of the body, and the life everlasting.'[27]

---

25 Coverdale's translation from the Book of Common Prayer.

26 This approach gives us a handle on what makes death 'wrong' and being dead 'unnatural'. C. S. Lewis put his finger on this when he noted that we find corpses uncanny, and if we were to see a disembodied soul (if ghosts exist, and if that is what they are), then we would find that uncanny too: and both because we 'hate the division which makes possible the conception of either corpse or ghost' (*Miracles*, London: Collins, 2012, p. 207).

27 Translation from *Common Worship: Services and Prayers for the Church of England*.

3

What is a Good Death?

William Caxton (*c.* 1420–92) was England's first printer. One of his earliest publications was a manual on *How to Die*, which remained a bestseller for two centuries. Preparation for death was taken seriously. In 1558, John Mere left a bequest for a sermon (the 'Mere Commemoration') to be preached every year to university students and fellows at Cambridge, the subject being the importance of preparing for death. The preacher, according to the will, 'shall exhort [the congregation] to the daily preparation of death and not to fear death otherwise than scripture doth allow'. Today, being on the receiving end of a sermon about the reality of death can be uncomfortable. In our culture, death is something to be held at arm's length. We try to avoid the idea, indeed the certainty, that death awaits each of us in the end. In the words of Richard Chartres, Bishop of London, there is a tendency today 'to gloss over the fact of death' that goes further than talking with euphemisms and excluding children from funerals. Evasion of death, as Chartres puts it, is also found in our 'hectic style of life [which] owes much to the suppressed fear of death and the unexamined notion that the faster we live, the more we shall get out of this short life'.[1]

The Christian idea of a 'good death' can appear stranger than ever against the backdrop of the secular outlook that we all share to some degree, within the Church and without. A 'good death' would mean one that we have prepared for: one that we meet, as

---

1 June 2003, in his president's lecture for the King's Fund. Quoted in Julia Neuberger, 'A Healthy View of Dying', *British Medical Journal*, 327 (2003), pp. 207–8.

far as we are able, with Christian faith. Since none of us knows when death will come, preparation for the inevitable is not something to be left for a recognized 'final stage' of life. If we are to be ready, as far as we are able, preparation must be part of the mainstream of Christian life and practice.

Chartres makes the provocative suggestion that a 'good death' is a 'healthy' one, which is to say, a death marked by wholeness, dignity and a sense of perspective. The Latin word for health is *salus*, which is also the root of our word 'salvation'. A good, or healthy, death is one placed firmly in the saving plans of God. As the bishop puts it, 'medical intervention is subservient to exploring the potential in dying for health – health defined as the sustaining and development of a personal identity nourished by the resources and challenges of the environment and, most importantly, our multidimensional relationships'.

Medical considerations

There is no 'one size fits all' checklist for a good *death*, just as there is no such checklist for how to *live*. We can, however, point to some overarching principles, which appear to be relatively uniform across variations in age, outlook and culture.

In 2003, the *British Medical Journal* conducted a poll among health workers and others to find out what they thought would constitute a good death. Of almost 700 people surveyed, over three-quarters cited freedom from unpleasant symptoms as the most important characteristic. Other principal hopes were choice over the place of their death, freedom from heroic medical interventions, and choice over timing of death.

In 1999, the UK-based charity Age Concern published a report entitled *The Future of Health and Care of Older People: The Best is Yet to Come*. It attempted to break the taboo on talking publicly about death, saying that death has been 'medicalised, professionalised and sanitised to such an extent that it is now alien to most people's daily lives'. The report set out 12 principles of a good death:

- To know when death is coming, and to understand what can be expected.
- To be able to retain control of what happens.
- To be afforded dignity and privacy.
- To have control over pain relief and other symptom control.
- To have choice and control over where death occurs (at home or elsewhere).
- To have access to information and expertise of whatever kind is necessary.
- To have access to any spiritual or emotional support required.
- To have access to hospice care in any location, not only in hospital.
- To have control over who is present and who shares the end.
- To be able to issue advance directives which ensure wishes are respected.
- To have time to say goodbye, and control over other aspects of timing.
- To be able to leave when it is time to go, and not to have life prolonged pointlessly.

From an American perspective, in 2000 the *Journal of the American Medical Association* reported similar concerns.[2] Factors, in order of importance, were listed as freedom from pain, peace with God, the presence of family, mental awareness, treatment that followed the patient's choices, having finances in order, a feeling that life was meaningful, a sense of resolved conflicts, and death at home. Patients placed a high value on attention to spirituality at the end of life, and in particular, on the importance of coming to peace with God and having opportunity for prayer. In fact, peace with God and pain control had nearly identical rankings for both patients and bereaved family members. The only difference was that some put an emphasis on a social and interpersonal context to their relation for God, whereas others saw this as a more private affair.

---

2 K. E. Steinhauser, 'Factors Considered Important at the End of Life by Patients, Family, Physicians, and other Care Providers', *Journal of the American Medical Association*, 284 (2000), pp. 2476–82.

A study conducted in Uganda among patients dying from AIDS, cancer, or both, revealed similar themes, despite vast cultural differences.[3] Three main needs were identified: the control or relief of pain and other symptoms, counselling, and financial assistance for the basic needs of their dependants, such as food, shelter and school fees. The preferred place of care, again, was home. Much of this evidence affirms Chartres' view that while medical care is vitally important, a good death involves more.

If we have a part to play in helping a death be a good one, we can begin by talking and listening to those who are dying. This might involve hearing the stories that surround the diagnosis of a terminal illness and the knowledge of impending death. We can seek to understand what this means for those concerned and what fears, hopes and desires it elicits. The research surveyed above suggests some of what those issues might be. However, everyone will have a particular slant on what these priorities should look like. We are unlikely to be in a position to help address all these needs. All the same, the more that those involved in the care of the dying are open to such discussions, the better those deaths will be. Clergy, doctors, carers – we may not get things right all the time, but what bereaved families tend to remember is that people cared, that they were honest and that they tried their best.

Preparing for death over the course of life

It is easy to imagine many reasons why contemporary culture does not encourage us to think about the certainty of our own death: it offends against the myth of progress that lies at the heart of the secular approach, and although scientific progress cannot deliver us from death, we seek to retain a sense of being in control. Death stands at odds with a cult of health and beauty; death is a metaphysical matter, and our culture leaves us feeling inarticulate and

---

3 E. Kikule, 'A Good Death in Uganda: Survey of Needs for Palliative Care for Terminally Ill People in Urban Areas', *British Medical Journal*, 327 (2003), p. 192.

ill prepared in such territory. Christians might attempt to buck these trends as individuals, but if we are to get very far, we will do well to attempt to buck them together. That calls for all of us, clergy and laity together, to try to find ways to bring reflection on death back into the life of the Church in a healthy, robust and constructive way.

We may begin by noticing that reflection on death is not entirely absent from church traditions. Churches that mark Ash Wednesday as the first day of Lent have a particularly striking tool at hand. First the priest and then members of the congregation receive the sign of the cross on their foreheads, traced in dark ash, accompanied by these or similar words: 'Remember that you are dust, and to dust you shall return. Turn away from sin and be faithful to Christ.' This service presents an ideal opportunity for Christians to think sensibly about death and their own mortality, and to do so within the safety of a liturgical framework.[4] Lent is a good time to reflect on our mortality and God's faithfulness; Ash Wednesday is a good time to begin.

Another avenue for reflection is provided by our older church buildings and churchyards, as places of burial and memorial. We might take this for granted, but the location of the remains of the dead already reveals something important about Christian hope and the belief that Christ has overcome the sting of death. The French scholar Philippe Ariès (1914–84) described three stages in Western history over the burial of the dead.[5] In the ancient pre-Christian world, corpses were considered to be unclean and were therefore buried outside the city walls. Christians felt no such fear or revulsion; indeed, they particularly revered the bodies of those who had given their lives as martyrs for Christ, and buried them in their churches, or built churches over their graves. As Ariès pointed out, this was a profound break with the practices of the pagan world, and an excellent indication of the extent to which

4 Ash Wednesday is a holy day when parishes of the Church of England are required to celebrate the Eucharist. The special provision for the day has been published in *Common Worship: Times and Seasons* (London: Church House Publishing, 2006). It is also available at <www.churchofengland.org>.
5 For instance in *The Hour of Our Death* (New York: Knopf, 1981).

Christ was seen to have 'tamed' death. In the modern, newly secular period, however, we see a reversion to the ancient pagan practice: municipal burial grounds tend to be situated away from centres of everyday life.

This story could be told in our churches as a way to introduce a Christian discussion of death. We could also turn to the graves and memorials in our own churches and churchyards. George Herbert (1593–1633) wrote about this in a characteristically knotty poem entitled 'Church Monuments'. He invites us to meditate upon the monuments and memorial stones found on the walls of parish churches. He calls such contemplation a 'school', which teaches us a lesson 'written in dusty heraldry and lines'. Mark the inscriptions, he writes, and remember the bodies, now turned to dust, which they commemorate. He pushes the image further: they are dust, like the sand in an hourglass measuring out our own span. Further still, even the monuments themselves will one day decay, but while they stand we can remember that we too stand before God like dust, like ashes.

At the heart of a healthy and robust preparation for death is a similar attitude towards life. When he was Archbishop of Canterbury, the theologian Rowan Williams once described the task of the Church as teaching people to pray and teaching them to die.[6] There is a link between the two. Prayer marks the orientation of our lives. Prayer means that our lives are more about God than they are about work, for instance, and are measured by concerns beyond pleasure and success. These are lessons to learn before we die. Every moment that we pray is, of course, worthwhile in itself, but prayer is also worthwhile in terms of the orientation it sets for our life, and what a life that has been frequently punctuated by prayer comes to mean overall: a life where prayer and remembrance of God have become a habit.

---

6 Address to Young Priest Theologians, Lambeth Palace, 15 October 2012. With this comment, Williams was picking up a theme expressed in the bishop's 'charge' to candidates for ordination as laid out in the *Common Worship* ordination service: 'They [priests] are to minister to the sick and prepare the dying for their death.'

Teaching people how to pray and how to die: we can explore this connection further. Both Rowan Williams and the much loved Cardinal Basil Hume, Archbishop of Westminster, have described prayer, in a deliberately shocking manner, as a monumental waste of time. That is, prayer contradicts, even defies, the contemporary assumption that we only spend time on that which brings measurable outcomes. This is the same drive that draws people away from leisure and play. Prayer reminds us that human beings, and time itself, have an intrinsic meaning, beyond productivity. What matters most are our relationships, with one another and with God. We do not need to be productive sources of measurable output in order to be meaningful.

In this way, prayer can be seen as being like leisure or play: it is its own justification. When we lose sight of this we lose sight of the purpose of life. If someone has worth only through what she achieves or produces, in the end she will be deemed worthless. At death (and indeed before that), she will cease to achieve or produce. Since Christians think differently about people, work, prayer and leisure, they should also think differently about death.[7] Christian preparation for death is a good vantage point from which to consider what it means to live. Preparation for death is about putting things in perspective. Far from being a morbid preoccupation, it can and should lead to a balanced, intentional and gratitude-filled appreciation of life. In the words of the Methodist writer J. Neville Ward (1915–92), 'Death helps us to see what is worth trusting and loving and what is a waste of time.'[8] Or to quote Pope Paul VI (1897–1978), 'Somebody should tell us, right at the start of our lives, that we are dying. Then we might live life to the limit, every minute of every day. Do it! I say. Whatever you want to do, do it now! There are only so many tomorrows.'[9]

---

7 On leisure, a great book of the twentieth century was Josef Pieper's *Leisure: The Basis for Culture*, translated by Alexander Dru with an introduction by T. S. Eliot (London: Faber and Faber, 1952).

8 J. Neville Ward, *Five for Sorrow, Ten for Joy: Meditations on the Rosary* (New York: Church Publishing, 2005), p. 97.

9 Quoted by Elizabeth Scalia, *Caring for the Dying with the Help of Your Catholic Faith* (Huntington: Our Sunday Visitor Publishing, 2008), p. 29.

Living mindful of our death prompts us to remember that life has a point. There is something to find: a pearl of great price. Or rather, there is *someone* to find (and he has found us). In words attributed to St Bernard of Clairvaux, it is to realize this: 'Life is only for love; time is only that we may find God.'

4

Self-Care

Among all the activities that human beings undertake, care of the dying is one of the most rewarding and necessary. It is also one of the most demanding, and potentially among the most draining. We should acknowledge the impact such ministry has on those who serve. Giving needs to be balanced by replenishing. Sadly, those in caring roles are often least good at caring for themselves. Those who care risk adopting a manner of life where they give without the counterbalance of restoration. This is not good for them nor, in the long term, is it good for those for whom they care.

'Self-care' may contain the word 'self' but that does not make it selfish. In the first place, as we have just noted, if we are to be effective in caring for others, it will be essential to look after ourselves. Beyond that, we care for people because of our sense of the immeasurable worth that each person has in the eyes of God. The person whom God has, more than any other, put into our hands to be alert for is *ourselves*. The Abbé de Tourville, a nineteenth-century Christian guide, offered good advice in *Letters of Spiritual Direction*, when he urged his readers to care for themselves with the same attention they would give to another.[1] Here, learning to step back and gain some perspective is important: it is to treat oneself objectively; it is to treat 'oneself as another', as Paul Ricoeur put it.[2]

Those who care for the dying need to cultivate a certain disposition, which we might call toughness or, better still, resilience.

---

1 Henri de Tourville, *Letters of Direction* (New York: Crowell, 1959).

2 Paul Ricoeur, *Oneself as Another* (Chicago: University of Chicago Press, 1992).

This is particularly vital if care for the dying is our daily work. Resilience is also necessary for those for whom ministry to the dying is new and perhaps only undertaken on an occasional basis. They are, almost by definition, less prepared. With that in mind, we suggest a ten-point plan to promote resilience in those involved in the care of the dying.[3] Any unfamiliar terms are discussed below. We would recommend the list to anyone going into full-time work with the dying, and we offer it here for readers for whom this ministry may be only part of what they do, since we think that the principles apply to pastoral ministry more generally.

1. Attend to physical needs.
2. Seek, celebrate and nurture meaningful relationships.
3. Face reality with support.
4. 'Reframe'.
5. Set goals.
6. Put an emphasis on good communication and obtain all necessary information.
7. Attend to spirituality.
8. Develop the 'creative art of coping'.
9. Do not be afraid of a sense of humour, and keep opportunities for laughter.
10. Seek to forgive and be forgiven.[4]

This list is basic, but that is no bad thing: that which is most basic is often the best place to start. With that in mind, it may be a good idea to begin with care of our *physical needs*. The same principles

---

3 This section is based on research carried out by Sioned. Since this work, our understanding of this field has been augmented by research from a team at St Christopher's Hospice, published by Barbara Monroe and David Oliviere as *Resilience in Palliative Care: Achievement in Adversity* (Oxford: Oxford University Press, 2007). The work on which some of this chapter is based was carried out by Sioned to look at promoting resilience among palliative care patients. However, it soon became apparent that the same list also applied to the carers and professionals involved.

4 For some pastoral wisdom from the thirteenth century, consider Thomas Aquinas' list of 'remedies of pain or sorrow': pursue something that makes you happy, do not be afraid to cry, seek out the company and sympathy of friends, contemplate the truth of divine things, and pay attention to body in all of this: have a bath and plenty of sleep, he suggests (*Summa Theologiae* II-I.38).

apply as much as they do for any other demanding pastoral work and they are common sense: make time for eating breakfast, lunch and dinner; sleep as much as you can; be careful about how much alcohol you drink; take regular exercise. We can easily let these building blocks slip in favour of more and more work but we cannot be our best for others if we are hungry, sleep-deprived and stressed. In a role where boundaries are ill-defined, there is all the more need to attend to boundaries over use of time, so that the role can be sustainable.

Make time to be with people whose relationships you treasure, and sustain those relationships. Beware being left with nothing to give to those who are closest to us. In this, we can learn from the very people to whom we are ministering: those who are dying. When we speak to people in this situation we hear treasured stories of close relationships, not accounts of what salary someone earned or how high they made it on the ladder of their career. We can learn from the dying about how to live, and nurture relationships now.

Good supervision and support are extremely important. We will stress this theme throughout our book. The reality is that some of the situations we encounter in ministering to the dying are upsetting, demanding and challenging. In the short term, we can stifle our reactions but this is not sustainable and not a good solution even in the medium term. With that in mind, find colleagues and other people whose wisdom you trust, who can listen and suggest guidance. (Questions of confidentiality, of course, are important.) People who care with resilience are not ultimately those who adopt the approach of a 'stiff upper lip', nor those who look on seeking support as a weakness.

Supervision and similar conversations will often involve working through what we are experiencing. This is sometimes approached in terms of *reframing*. A large body of evidence suggests that *how* we perceive a stress or adversity affects our subsequent thoughts and behaviour, and therefore the ultimate effect of that experience. Just as it is enormously helpful to encourage patients and relatives to see their situation in a different light, this is also often helpful for those who minister to them. For instance, we can ask ourselves, or have others explore with us, the quite specific question of what it means to view the situation from the perspective of Christian faith, or as someone working as part of a team.

Similarly, *goal setting* fosters hope and perspective. That can be as simple as committing ourselves to getting to bed by a certain time or taking up a new hobby or resolution. Achieving a goal, or even simply working towards it, can promote a sense of worth that helps build resilience during difficult times.

Another theme of this book is *communication*. We can all work on this, not only in relation to those for whom we care but also in relation to those who support us, and with our colleagues. Simply having information is important: we can easily feel out of control if we are aware of being 'out of the loop' or uninformed.

When we asked one hospice chaplain about self-care, his first answer was to point to the importance of a strong prayer life. Nothing substitutes for some sense of daily retreat: of time for prayer, away from the demands of ministry, even if only momentarily so. We might think about getting away from our place of work for replenishment on a more formal retreat from time to time. They can last for as little as a day to, sometimes, as long as a month.[5]

The *creative art of coping* refers to that which we do that is totally removed from our work. Hobbies, fun, recreation – whatever we call it – are an escape from the demands of ministry.[6] They provide time devoted to doing something that brings enjoyment and refreshment. For some people this is sport, for others knitting, for others photography. An important aspect of contentment is finding something in which one can 'lose oneself', as for instance when we lose the sense of time passing.

Much research has confirmed the link between humour and well-being. A sense of humour is often counted as an essential component of ministry. Clergy, in particular, among themselves,

---

5 The pattern proposed by St Ignatius of Loyola was for 30 days in its full form, although shorter versions are more popular today.

6 The significance for well-being of creativity and working with our hands has been explored recently by Richard Sennett in *The Craftsman* (London: Penguin, 2009) and by Matthew B. Crawford in *The Case for Working with your Hands, or, Why Office Work is Bad for Us and Fixing Things Feels Good* (London: Viking, 2009).

can resort to some fairly dark humour. While it is important to retain a sense of the right time for this, and the right place, we cannot always be meeting death and suffering with complete seriousness.

Carrying the burden of un-forgiveness can eat away at us. 'Forgive yourself before you die; then forgive others', was the advice of Morrie Schwartz, an American professor of sociology, and the subject of the best-selling book *Tuesdays with Morrie*,[7] written as he died from ALS or motor neurone disease. 'Seek the forgiveness of God', we might add. Resilience is built from the freedom that forgiveness brings. That is not to say that forgiveness is easy, and it may only be through prayer and wise counsel that we learn how it can be possible.

Our own mortality

One way to be in a good position to serve the dying is to give attention to our own mortality. As we noted in the previous chapter, we live in a society in which it is very easy to hide from death. Throughout this book we celebrate the strides that have been made in palliative care in past decades, but we should concede that they have contributed to the trend by which death usually takes place outside the home. Although we might sometimes mock the prudery of the Victorians, we have our own taboo topics, and death is one of them. Even in church, death and dying are not often topics for sermons or study groups.

In Chapter 2 we discussed the sense that no one need feel ashamed about fearing death. For all that Christians subscribe to a faith with a hope of eternal life, many of us fear death, and that includes clergy and lay ministers. Faith, hope and fear are not necessarily in tension: the sense of 'bad news' about death is part of what makes Christ's victory – which we hope to share – such good news. We receive that hope but we recognize that it does not rescue us from dying.

---

7 Mitch Albom, *Tuesdays with Morrie: An Old Man, a Young Man and Life's Greatest Lesson* (New York: Doubleday, 1997).

We may well fear *dying* more than we fear 'being dead'. That is reasonable. We might also feel unease at not knowing quite what process or state awaits us between death and the final judgement. Hope, after all, concerns matters as yet not fully comprehended.[8] Such self-reflection will help us to realize what it is we could most usefully talk over with a spiritual director, for instance. It will also help us to sympathize with the concerns of others, not least of those who are dying.

Films and books, both fiction and non-fiction, can be a good catalyst or provocation for self-examination.[9] We have already mentioned retreats, and if work with the dying is to become a mainstay of our ministry, it is worth thinking about making a guided retreat, with someone to talk to each day, as a time away to meditate and reflect on death and dying in light of Christ's life and the resurrection. It is worth being honest and asking questions such as, 'What is it that I fear in death?' You may find it useful to make a will and plan your own funeral, as part of this, and – as we have already said – in all of this to reflect on the experience with someone else.

Most clergy will have visited a funeral director's premises and been 'behind the scenes' at a crematorium. A lay visitor may not have had these experiences. Such visits can be emotionally demanding but they can also be useful, especially if they are set within a context of prayer, reflection and supervision. Many hospital or hospice chaplains welcome conversations with parish clergy and lay visitors. It may even be possible to spend a day alongside one.

---

8 Aristotle wrote that a little knowledge of the highest things, which are the hardest to grasp, such as *divine things*, is worth more than fuller knowledge of lower matters. We might extrapolate from this and say that even if hope is shrouded in mystery when it comes to life beyond death, such hope is of greater worth than complete transparency would be over something more trivial.

9 Among books, for instance, C. S. Lewis, *A Grief Observed*, Ruth Picardie, *Before I Say Goodbye*, Michael Mayne, *Enduring Melody*, Richard Payne and John Swinton, *Living Well* and *Dying Faithfully*, Jean-Dominique Bauby, *The Diving-Bell and the Butterfly*, and Anthony Wilson, *Riddance* (a collection of poems). Among films, we might consider *Shadowlands*, *Iris*, *Whose Life is it Anyway?*, *The Bucket List*, *Dying Young* and *Life Before Death*, an award-winning documentary series on end of life issues.

5

The Dying Person

At the heart of the contemporary approach to palliative care lies the concept of 'total pain'. As we saw in Chapter 1, it was proposed by Dame Cicely Saunders and takes into account all the struggles the dying person faces: physical, psychological, social, spiritual and practical.[1] Such an appreciation of the complex and multi-dimensional nature of suffering is one reason why Saunders' work is so significant. It means that palliative care does not simply focus on the immediate physical manifestations of the life-curtailing illness. We are emotional and spiritual beings, and these aspects play their part in the process of dying. Since everyone is unique, each individual's experiences will be different, depending not only on the illness but on family circumstances and the person's emotional and spiritual state. In this chapter we consider various aspects of 'total pain', turning first to look at some of the common physical symptoms that dying people experience. We should stress that while we might look at different aspects in turn, that does not mean that these aspects are cut off from one another: the holistic vision sees them as interconnected.

Common physical symptoms

Physical pain

No one wants to be in pain, and controlling pain is a high priority in looking after a dying person. Care for spiritual well-being

1 Caroline Richmond, 'Obituary: Dame Cicely Saunders', *British Medical Journal*, 331 (2005), p. 238.

and emotional welfare is very difficult when someone is in severe physical discomfort. We might try to recall a time when we have been in pain and remember how all-encompassing it was, and how difficult it was to focus on anything else.

The management of pain has advanced significantly in the past half-century. One of the arts of pain management is to identify what is causing the pain and then use the appropriate painkillers (also called analgesics) to ease it, since different types of pain require different medicines.

Broadly speaking, pain is classified into three types. One is damage to soft tissue (nociceptive pain), which can be caused by anything from a bruise to a tumour. Then there is damage to muscles and joints (musculoskeletal pain) and, finally, there is pain from damage to nerves (neuropathic pain).

With damage to soft tissue, the first step will be the use of paracetamol (called acetaminophen in the USA). If the pain is more severe, a weak member of the opiate family of painkillers will be used (such as codeine), progressing to a stronger variety, such as morphine. (Opioids are a related class of painkillers.) Common side-effects of opiates are nausea, vomiting and constipation. Confusion and hallucinations can occur if the dosage is too high for the patient. Strong opiates can be given by a variety of means, depending on what is best for the individual. Those who can swallow can be given tablets or liquid. An alternative for those who cannot is a lollipop-like 'lozenge', which the patient can suck, or a dissolvable tablet that is put under the tongue. A patch, placed on the skin, is another method. Another option is a device called a syringe driver, which can also be used to administer morphine, or other medications: a small pump releases a regular amount of medication from a syringe through a small needle placed under the skin. You may see the pump beside a bed, or a patient wearing one in a purpose-made bag that hangs around the neck. This is an excellent way to give medication to patients who cannot swallow, who are nauseated and vomiting, or who are too weak to manage oral medications. The syringe is typically replenished every 24 hours.

Musculoskeletal pain is treated with a group of drugs called

NSAIDs (non-steroidal anti-inflammatory drugs). Examples of these are ibuprofen and diclofenac. They can cause indigestion, so they may not be suitable for some patients, for example those with a history of stomach ulcers. Equally, they can be toxic to the kidneys, so they are often avoided or at least used cautiously in patients at risk of kidney failure. For those who can take them, they tend to be highly effective.

Neuropathic (nerve) pain is one of the most difficult pains to treat. A common example of this type of pain is sciatica. There are oral painkillers designed to target this type of nerve pain (such as amitriptyline and gabapentin), often used in conjunction with opiates.

Dame Cicely wrote in the *Nursing Mirror* that 'constant pain needs constant control'.[2] This principle has been borne out by far more sophisticated research than she was able to perform. Taking analgesics at regular intervals prevents peaks of pain, keeping it at a more controllable level. Modern medicine has attempted to make this simpler by introducing slow-release tablets, which need only be taken twice per day.

Another important principle is that a person should have additional doses prescribed when necessary: so-called 'breakthrough' painkillers. These are given on top of the background dose of regular medication, for those situations when the pain 'breaks through'.

It is imperative that any plan of medication (sometimes called the regime) is reviewed regularly. This applies to all medication, not just to that for pain control. A nominated professional will oversee the dosing and monitoring of its effects. This helps to prevent the situation where someone is under- or overmedicated, or misses an opportunity to try medication that might suit him better.

Concerns have sometimes been raised over the risk that a dying person may become dependent on opiate drugs, such as morphine. This fear makes some patients, and their families, keen to avoid these medicines. These worries can be allayed. If the best prin-

2 Shirley Du Boulay and Marianne Rankin, *Cicely Saunders: The Founder of the Modern Hospice Movement* (London: SPCK, 2007), p. 47.

ciples are adhered to, such as prescribing a dose appropriate for the pain and monitoring the situation, 'dependence' is unlikely to occur. By far the greatest reason for increasing dosages of opiates is that the disease is progressing and that greater pain relief is therefore required. For some other medicines, a risk of dependence might have been a concern if the patient were not in the final stage of life. If, however, it is clear that death is approaching, dependence is no longer an important consideration, while the desire to control symptoms remains very much so.

We sometimes encounter the idea that the use of painkillers can make someone die sooner, perhaps coupled with the view that this is acceptable since that is not the primary intention of the doctor who prescribes the medicine. The facts do not seem to bear this out. Used responsibly, for the control of pain, these medicines do not accelerate death.[3]

Nausea and vomiting

As with the experience of being in pain, nausea can be extremely debilitating. It is a common symptom and has many causes, depending upon the diagnosis. Again, the physician's role is to identify the cause and begin the appropriate treatment. Anti-nausea medications are known as anti-emetics. They can be given by mouth, but the syringe driver route described above can be a very useful way to administer them.

When the nausea or vomiting are caused by an obstruction from a tumour high up in the bowel, for example, often the only way to ease the symptoms is to insert a naso-gastric tube. This tube is inserted via a nostril and runs down the back of the throat to sit in the stomach. It can be left to drain freely so that the contents of the stomach pass up into a bag attached to the tube. It is possible that a dying person will find relief from having one of these inserted, although some people find them uncomfortable around the nostril. These tubes are more usally used for the opposite role: for feeding as opposed to drainage. The issue of

3 Rob George and Claud Regnard, 'Lethal opioids or dangerous prescribers?', *Palliative Medicine*, 21 (2007), pp. 77–80.

artificial feeding and hydration of a dying person will be discussed in a later chapter.

Breathlessness

A dying patient may be short of breath for several reasons, depending on the underlying diagnosis. A chest infection is a common cause. People who are dying are prone to such infections because they have weaker defences to fight off infections and they are often sedentary or bed-bound. As a cause of death, pneumonia used to be known as 'the old man's friend'. Death from pneumonia was thought to be relatively peaceful: that is, in a painless, semi-conscious state. This may be the case for some, but it is more likely that a person will require medication to ease the symptoms, and breathlessness can be frightening.

Lung tumours also cause breathlessness. A primary lung tumour is a cancer that originated in the lungs. Secondary tumours (also known as metastases) can spread to the lungs from another site, where the cancer first occurred: for example, from a primary breast or bowel cancer. As the tumour, or tumours, in the lung grow, the amount of healthy lung tissue diminishes and the patient will become increasingly breathless. This is also the case in chronic lung diseases such as emphysema. Breathlessness can also be caused by heart failure. As the heart is not able to pump effectively, liquid collects (or 'pools') in the lungs.

Some people in the last days or hours of life can develop a very 'rattly chest', which is sometimes unfortunately known as the 'death rattle'. This is caused by a combination of an inability to cough, usually because the patient is unconscious, and secretions in the lungs and upper airways. Although the patient is not likely to be conscious at this stage, it can be very distressing for the carers looking on. The drug hyoscine is often administered to dry the secretions, via a syringe driver. This is more effective the earlier it is given. The same drug also has a beneficial sedative effect.

Breathlessness is frequently accompanied by fear and anxiety. People have described it as 'a fear of drowning' or 'running out of breath'. All of us can relate to the panic that we would feel at not being able to breathe properly. Medication is therefore accompanied by strategies that provide reassurance and calm. Non-medical visitors can help here. Simple suggestions to help someone to feel more comfortable breathing include the following:

- Encourage the person to sit upright.
- Talk calmly.
- Try to create a peaceful environment, although this is often difficult on a busy hospital ward.
- Find a relaxing 'distraction', whether that be music, prayer or company.

Medications can be given to ease breathlessness, such as small regular doses of oral liquid morphine or doses of benzodiazepines (sedative medication) such as diazepam (and sometimes both), to help with anxiety. Relaxation exercises are often recommended, perhaps accompanied by music or a video. Antibiotics may be given to treat a chest infection if the person is well enough to take medication by mouth. We will return to this subject in Chapter 9 when we consider the topic of withholding and withdrawing life-sustaining treatment.

Other common symptoms

We have looked in detail at three of the most frequent symptoms people may experience and which you may therefore encounter: pain, nausea and breathlessness. We are not writing a medical textbook, so other symptoms are not considered in such detail, but we can highlight some additional information that may be helpful to know when alongside a person who is dying.

Bowel disturbance is not uncommon. Some patients experience diarrhoea, others severe constipation. Incontinence of faeces can be an embarrassing and debilitating problem. A medical assessment will try to establish the cause and aim to alleviate the problem. Some patients who have had bowel surgery to bypass a blockage will have a stoma bag. Urinary catheters are common for people who are bed-bound and find it difficult to get to the toilet or onto a commode. A drainage bag may be evident on a small stand at floor level.

Poor appetite is a natural phenomenon when we are dying. Relatives often struggle with this, since 'feeding up' is associated with getting stronger. Cartons of nutritious drinks may be favoured over a meal on a plate. They can be sipped over the course of the day.

Fatigue is very common. Practically speaking, this means that activities need to be carefully paced. This might apply even to having conversations, and to the number of visitors someone can cope with seeing. For the patient, the feeling can be similar to the exhaustion we experience when we have the flu. We need to be sensitive to the need for rest and peace.

Changes in appearance

Both an illness and its treatment can result in physical changes to the patient. This can be one of the hardest things to face or come to terms with, both for the patient and for family members who may also struggle with these changes. The husband who was always physically strong, and was relied upon for physical tasks, may now be painfully thin and in need of assistance to go to the toilet. Changes in appearance can be a constant and painful reminder of the loss that has already occurred and of the frustration and sorrow of not being able to reverse the inevitable.

Hair loss can occur with some chemotherapy. This can include eyelashes, eyebrows and pubic hair. Hair loss also occurs at the site of radiotherapy treatment to the head, with perhaps some loss at the opposite side too, where the radiotherapy beam has passed through. Both men and women tend to struggle with this change in their appearance. Wigs can work for some people, but not all; scarves and hats may be preferred. Most hospitals will have access to a specialist advisory service regarding wig and scarf fittings. Some charities have 'make-over' days, which can provide a much needed pampering service to boost self-esteem. Hair does grow back following completion of treatment such as chemotherapy, but is often different – sometimes curlier, sometimes a different colour. Hair should be fully regrown by four to six months following chemotherapy. It often takes longer for hair to grow back following radiotherapy and sometimes the loss is permanent.

Long-term usage of steroid tablets will also result in changes in appearance. (These are not the anabolic or 'body-building' steroids we might otherwise associate with the word. Steroids are a broad class of chemicals and perform all sorts of roles in the body.) Some illnesses require a high dose of steroids in order to control symptoms, despite the potential side-effects. Brain tumours are one such condition. Often there is swelling around the tumour (cerebral oedema), which can result in raised pressure within the skull. This can cause terrible headaches and vomiting or, at worst, seizures and reduced consciousness. Steroid treatment reduces the swelling around the tumour and relieves these symptoms. A person who has been on steroids for several weeks will start to gain significant weight around their abdomen, however, and develop facial swelling. These changes can be a source of embarrassment for the person.

Long-standing hormone treatment for prostate cancer effectively diminishes levels of male hormones in the blood, so that men lose muscle and body hair, gain weight and may develop breasts. Such changes to appearance can have a significant psychological impact.

Swelling of the abdomen might also be caused by a tumour itself, if it is very large, or by the accumulation of fluid around the lining of the abdomen as a result of a tumour. This fluid is known as ascites and can be drained off. There can sometimes be several litres of fluid, which will re-accumulate over time. The swelling can give someone the shape of a heavily pregnant woman. It is a very obvious sign of their disease and can be distressing and uncomfortable: walking around can become difficult.

Head and neck tumours can be among the most disfiguring conditions, either because of the presence of the tumour itself or as a result of the surgery or radiotherapy involved in the treatment. A tumour involving the neck region may result in the need for a tracheostomy, which is a surgically created opening in the trachea (our main breathing tube from the mouth to the lungs), kept open by a plastic tube. A tracheostomy is performed when there is an obstruction in the upper airway that would prevent oxygen getting from the mouth to the lungs, for example from a tumour. Following surgery, air can pass through the tracheostomy tube directly into the trachea and into the lungs. A tracheostomy tube will affect the quality of the voice, and people may be limited to a whisper. Speaking can therefore be exhausting, although sometimes a valve can be used which makes speaking easier.

The change in appearance from 'what used to be' can be one of a series of losses that people encounter. It is useful to acknowledge this as loss and recognize that these changes play a large part in the emotional and psychological suffering that a dying person may be experiencing. Changes that may not be so visible but have still involved a loss would include a mastectomy (removal of one or both breasts) for breast cancer, a hysterectomy or an amputation now concealed by a false limb.

There can be unpleasant smells, perhaps from bowel disturbances, or from 'fungating' tumours: very advanced tumours that break through the skin, for instance with an advanced sinus tumour or an advanced breast cancer. Because they disrupt the skin, it begins to decay, which can produce an unpleasant odour. Certain dressings can reduce the odour, if the tumour is on the outside of the body. Incense burners can also help. It is truly an act of love to sit alongside someone in this situation. Try to separate the smell from the human being. Often people will avoid these patients, and this can be read as rejection at a time when they are greatly in need.

Emotional, psychological and social suffering

A focus on the physical component of suffering is not enough. What Sheila Cassidy said of doctors applies to Christian visitors as well: 'We have to learn to be whole person doctors because our patients are whole persons.'[4] We are *whole persons*, who think,

---

4 Sheila Cassidy, *Sharing the Darkness: The Spirituality of Caring* (London: Darton, Longman & Todd, 1988), p. 16.

feel and relate. This makes human suffering not only multi-dimensional but also interconnected. Up to this point, this chapter has concentrated on the most immediately physical needs of the dying person, but we do not want to isolate this dimension of the person and her suffering. One aspect influences the others. We now turn to emotional suffering, which can be thought of as centred around two major components: loss and fear.

Loss

Throughout the course of a life-threatening illness, a series of losses will be encountered which, in their own way, become a series of bereavements. These losses can take many forms: physical, social, practical or spiritual. Those who care for and love the dying person will also be experiencing their own losses, each from their own perspective.

Loss involves the loss of both *what has been* and *what could have been*. By 'what has been', we mean losing what has been enjoyed up until now. The impact of this loss varies for different individuals, depending on their circumstances and illness. As we have already noted, the loss of physical appearance or ability can result in feelings of frustration or anger or a sense of inadequacy. Then there is the loss of the role we play in society. Those of working age may have had to give up their jobs, with the associated financial implications. We are often defined by our jobs or roles, rightly or wrongly. Being unable to continue with these can leave someone with a loss of identity. The sick person might ask, 'Who am I, if I no longer perform this role?'

Loss of paid employment is not the only consideration here. Not being able to fulfil a role in the home or in a local club or church can be equally devastating. Couples who have worked well together over the years, perhaps with clearly defined roles, have to adapt to a new way of living, and this can be a considerable challenge. Roles may be reversed, and the one who has always done the shopping and the cooking has to relinquish those tasks to someone who has never learned to do them. This can be awkward.

Beyond this, there are unspoken, subconscious roles that we take on, such as the 'care-giver', the 'provider' and the 'one who copes', to name a few. At some point in the illness, these roles are given up. For the healthy partner, this can feel as if a gap is opening up, which begins to represent what life will be like in the future after that person has died. It highlights the strengths and gifts the person has and what those gifts have meant to others. As those gifts fade, a grieving process begins for what may have been taken for granted over the years.

The loss of 'what could have been' refers to losing one's future. 'Don't leave it all until your retirement,' patients are often heard to say. They speak from raw experience. When people die just before or after retirement, they leave many plans unfulfilled: plans representing future dimensions of a relationship that have been deferred, perhaps unwisely, during decades of all-consuming work.

Of all the losses of what could have been, most people find the prospect of leaving their families by far the hardest. Reflecting on what has mattered to them over the course of their lives, few people speak of their jobs, cars or bank balance; they speak instead of their families and friends. These are inherently the most precious parts of our lives, and their loss is the worst. This is never more poignant than when a young parent is dying, who will never see her children grow up, nor share in all that they will be and do in the future. Other patients speak of not being around to see an impending grandchild born, to see their children graduate, or simply to be there for their families, providing love and support.

One model of grief that has often been found to be helpful comes from Elisabeth Kübler-Ross, in her 1969 book *On Death and Dying*.[5] It is widely used not only to represent the emotional suffering encountered after a death has occurred, but also to understand the bereavement that is suffered by the dying person, and families and friends, *as death approaches.*

---

5 A 40th anniversary edition has been published with a new introduction by Professor Allan Kellehear: Elisabeth Kübler-Ross, *On Death and Dying: What the Dying have to Teach Doctors, Nurses, Clergy and their own Families* (London: Routledge, 2008).

The five stages of grief that Kübler-Ross describes are represented by the acronym DABDA: Denial, Anger, Bargaining, Depression and Acceptance. Kübler-Ross came to believe that not all these stages necessarily occur in every case, nor in this order. People do, however, usually experience at least two of them. Women are more likely than men to experience all five. It is common to move between or among the stages, maybe several times, before reaching the stage of acceptance. We will consider them each briefly.

Despite its negative connotations, *denial* can actually be quite a good coping mechanism in the short term. We can all recall times when we have denied that there is a problem in order to continue 'life as normal' and perhaps to avoid facing a difficult truth. We can convince ourselves that the particular problem is not really happening, and that all is fine, or that a solution will be found when none can reasonably be expected. In general, over time, this is replaced by a sense of realism.

Once denial has been acknowledged, and reality hits, it is quite natural for *anger* to be expressed, with questions such as 'Why me?' and 'What have I ever done to deserve this?' There can also be a desire to blame someone for what is happening. This anger is usually misplaced or misdirected, but at times may be appropriate. People may be angry at themselves for the situation in which they find themselves, so guilt may also play a part. People may be angry towards God. At this stage, a listening ear is most useful, and willingness simply to witness the anger. Attempts to rationalize what a person is going through are unlikely to be constructive at this stage. It is important, however, that the person is able to move through this stage, as it is very difficult to care for someone who is angry. We tend to take our anger out on those closest to us and those who are providing most care. On that account, it can be important to take time also to listen to those carers. The anger may be directed at the minister or visitor, and if you are in this role it is important to see this as a natural stage of grief, rather than a personal attack.

The third stage – *bargaining* – often accompanies the recognition that death is approaching (if, as here, we apply this model to an impending death), but combined with the hope that there may still be a 'way out', or at least some means of gaining more time. This is often directed at a 'Higher Power'. This can suggest an innate awareness that we are not in control of our destiny or the timing of our death. Such appeals for more time are put into words with phrases such as, 'I'd do anything if only I could only ...' or 'I'd give up everything I own to ...' Parents of dying children, of all ages, will plead to be able to exchange places, so that their children may have the life they themselves have already lived or expect in the future.

The stage of *depression* represents acceptance of the reality that death is inevitable, despite anger and despite pleas for more time. There can be a sense that life is not worth living unless we are healthy and 'fully functioning'. At this stage the dying person or their loved ones will naturally be tearful and withdrawn. The dying person may feel a huge burden because he sees those around him struggling and suffering. It is important to allow appropriate sadness to be expressed. That said, depression in another can be hard to witness. It is far easier to avoid these discussions or to try to convince someone that, actually, all is well.

At the last stage, *acceptance*, peace is found. There is an understanding that the inevitable will happen but that 'it is going to be OK'. Some sense is being made of the situation; people are coming to terms with mortality. Acceptance is not opposed to grief: it is part of grief.

Grief is a natural response to loss; grieving is natural. However, we should recognize that some forms of grief are pathological: they lie outside the bounds of a normal response and are fundamentally unhelpful. Concerns may arise if the responses at any of the stages of grief appear extreme. A health professional might review the situation, since clinical depression, for example, can be treated. A doctor may be able to differentiate between what is an appropriate sadness in the face of a terminal diagnosis and what is, in effect, a treatable illness.

That judgement can be difficult. Often the features of clinical depression mimic symptoms of the illness itself. Lack of appetite, loss of energy and insomnia, for instance, are indicators of clinical depression but they are also very common symptoms among those who are terminally ill. However, profound withdrawal or tearfulness may be distinguishing features. Knowledge of the length and nature of the depression and of the person's usual personality can be helpful information for a medic deciding whether what is being experienced is part of the response to the illness or a treatable clinical depression.

Fear

The other significant driving factor in emotional distress is fear. As with loss, this can present itself in a variety of ways. The nature of the fear will also vary.

The hopes and desires for 'a good death', as explored in Chapter 3, line up with aspects of fear of dying 'badly'. For many, this would be dying in pain or with uncontrolled symptoms; for others it is about not having said goodbye; having a say over their place of death is a priority for others. Fear of being a burden on families and friends can also feature significantly.

Patients may be fearful of what lies beyond death. Those with a Christian faith have hope of eternal life shared with Christ, and that can be a comfort. Other religious traditions also offer hope. However, as we noted in Chapter 4, the idea of journeying to the unknown can be a daunting, and perhaps lonely, prospect even for those who hold a strong Christian faith. We cannot know what that will be like; there is no equivalent of an antenatal class to prepare us.

We mentioned loneliness, even though death is something all human beings share. The Christian tradition has always had a strong conviction that the journey from this life is one in which we are supported by the saints and the angels. Christians can be reassured that we die in the bosom of the Church, accompanied by the whole company of heaven. That does not excuse us from attending to Christian care and presence during the last hours of someone's life. Indeed, the practical Christian care and presence of the Church on earth is our reflection of the care and presence of the Church in heaven.

Someone with a more nihilistic view of death may ponder what life has been about. It seems understandable that people wonder how their family will fare without them. Some wonder if their life has amounted to anything. The thought of extinction – of non-existence – can be very troubling for those who see death this way. Others find it less of a problem since – and this is not a facetious point – they will not be there to experience what they perceive as their coming absence.

Alongside repetitive and troubled thoughts, and poor concentration, fears of all kinds can present themselves in physical ways through the symptoms of anxiety, which include disturbed sleep, pain, breathlessness and nausea.

A response to psychological and social pain

Doctors can prescribe medication in response to emotional distress. However, this should not be seen as a panacea, nor as a substitute for the progress that can be made on the basis of good communication. Drugs known as anxiolytics (which relieve anxiety) can provide some relief. These include diazepam, lorazepam and midazolam. These drugs have an addictive potential but when life expectancy is short this concern may not be particularly relevant. Listening is always useful, and all the more so when it is carried out according to the principles of 'active listening', which we outline in the next chapter.

No one care-giver will be in a position to address the whole constellation of problems and worries faced by the dying person. This makes the team approach to holistic care all the more important, and it can be useful for everyone involved with care of the dying to have a sense of what services are available. Some palliative care teams are fortunate to have a counsellor or a psychologist who can give specialist advice to patients and relatives who are struggling. Complementary therapists may offer massage and relaxation techniques. Art, music, poetry and gentle exercise can all bring relief, although they will not all necessarily be available and not every patient is equally willing to engage with them.

Just because a person is dying and may not leave hospital does not mean that practical household considerations are insignificant: far from it. The principal cause of anxiety may be worry for those who will be left behind, and this may focus around highly practical concerns, perhaps over housing or income. Social workers are trained to provide assistance with these matters and can fulfil an important role of liaison between the various parties involved.

Underpinning all this is the need to offer a compassionate response, regardless of role. In his book dedicated to the subject of compassion, the doctor Ralph Crawshaw describes it notably as follows: 'The experience of compassion does not pass from the lighted world to the retina inwardly, but from the enlightened heart outwardly as we venture to reach something more than ourself reflected.'[6] Compassion has been described as arising from 'an openness of heart, a willingness to understand other people's pain, to listen to their hurt and share in their distress'.[7] Some commentators have argued that this essential component is undermined in today's healthcare system, even to the extent that a lack of compassion can compromise the care of patients. We would prefer to say that few, if any, in healthcare have forgotten the significance of compassion, but that *time* with the patient, during which compassion can be shown most directly, has sometimes been limited, to the frustration of many. With that in mind, a renewed focus on the virtue of compassion is likely to be welcomed by all.[8]

Sometimes, caring for the dying can feel like a hopeless task, one in which we are impotent onlookers with no power to battle the force of the inevitable. However, we should remember that we have the opportunity to show compassion. We are then doing and offering something invaluable. As Dave Tomlinson puts it, 'Every

6 Ralph Crawshaw, *Compassion's Way: A Doctor's Quest into the Soul of Medicine* (Bloomington, IN: Medi-ed Press, 2002), p. 627.

7 Dave Tomlinson, *How to be a Bad Christian ... And a Better Human Being* (London: Hodder & Stoughton, 2012), p. 181.

8 As for instance suggested in the recent UK document *Compassion in Practice: Nursing, Midwifery and Care Staff – Our Vision and Strategy* (NHS Commissioning Services, December 2012).

single act of compassion is a flap of a butterfly's wings' – and the flap of a butterfly's wing in one place may lead to unknown consequences elsewhere: the so-called 'butterfly effect'. Tomlinson goes on: 'You may not see the final outcome, but keep flapping!'[9] The heart of this response comes down to how we *are* with dying people and the importance of good communication. The next chapter is dedicated to this topic.

Spiritual pain

As a final dimension, we consider what is sometimes called 'spiritual pain', a term that collects together some useful perspectives on suffering, such as the experience of guilt or of meaninglessness. The phrase also carries some considerable risks. In particular, we are not pointing to 'spiritual pain' as if it were somehow distinct and unrelated from other sorts of pain. The physical and the social are always already 'spiritual', so physical and social suffering are similarly spiritual. Matter, in the Christian vision, is inherently 'spiritual': it is significant to God; it is subject to his pronouncement of 'good', even 'very good', at the beginning of Genesis; it is the arena in which encounter with good and evil, with sin and redemption, is worked out.

Similarly, everything encompassed by the categories of 'emotional' and 'psychological' suffering is clearly also spiritual. Fear, for instance, is a 'spiritual' matter, whatever is feared.

The value of including 'spiritual pain' in an analysis of the 'total pain' experienced by a dying person is not to carve out an area that is 'spiritual' in contradistinction to what is otherwise acknowledged. The value, instead, is in making sure that certain parts of what it means to be human are not neglected.

Perhaps the most common and significant element included under 'spiritual pain' is guilt. In response to this, the Christian faith offers the possibility of forgiveness. That possibility is by no means something to be taken for granted. The promise of forgiveness offered by Christianity is something remarkable.

9 Tomlinson, *Bad Christian*, p. 181.

A sense of guilt might extend towards both God and other people, either as individuals or as a multitude that goes beyond individual figures. Both dimensions are important, and we will return to forgiveness in Chapter 8. We can stand by people as they seek forgiveness in each of these ways: to be reconciled to God and to be reconciled to others. In the last stage of life, our encounter with God's forgiveness can usefully be as concrete and tangible as possible. For that reason, many churches have stressed the value of making a formal confession, and receiving the formal absolution of the Church from a priest, as death approaches. The Church of England, for instance, comments on this in the Book of Common Prayer (in the service of the Visitation of the Sick). Confession at this stage of life is also stressed by the Orthodox Churches and the Roman Catholic Church. When we turn to God for forgiveness, God forgives. We do not need to be able to 'put it right'. Just as with the penitent thief, someone can be forgiven in his last hour. We could not ask for a stronger reminder that we are saved by grace, not works.[10]

A particular problem can be a sense of guilt for wrongdoings that cannot conceivably now be reconciled or resolved; perhaps the offended party has died, or is beyond contact in some other way, or perhaps we are aware that those we have harmed are too many or dispersed to be addressed. Here it may be helpful to note that theologians say that God's work of reconciliation extends to healing all the wounds in the communal body, and is not complete until all of the knots and entanglements in human relationships are worked free. A seemingly technical distinction in the Catholic theological tradition bears witness to this point: it is the distinction between 'guilt' and something else that we will call 'mess'. God is committed, on this view, to dealing with both: not only with guilt but also with mess. When it comes to guilt, as the hymn puts it, 'the foulest offender who truly believes that instant from Jesus a pardon receives' (although we might think that this formulation misses out the centrality of baptism). When it comes to the mess, the timescale is as long as needs be. God works with

---

10 Eph. 2.8–9.

the grain of creaturely existence, which is time-bound, and his work to heal and restore, and to sort out mess, may take a long time. This lies at the heart of the idea that God may have work to complete in each of us between death and the resurrection. Whatever we think about that point, the important notion is that God is concerned about those seemingly intractable broken relationships and seemingly irreparable effects of our wrongdoing. However intractable and irreparable they seem to us, God has them in view. We can commend ourselves to God, and commend each other to God, with the confidence that salvation reaches out to embrace all of these concerns.

Close to guilt lies regret. Very few of us are going to face our last days without regrets. The Christian message is fully realistic about this. Indeed, this forms the background against which the message of the gospel arrives with its full force, not least with the promise of Christ that he will renew all things: 'See, I am making all things new' (Rev. 21.5).

One regret may be that a person is only facing these questions late in the day, and indeed, she may be wondering whether there is still time, or scope, for a new, or renewed, relationship with God so close to 'the end'. Our response to this can be that the assurance that it is 'never too late' when it comes to God lies close to the heart of the gospel, being a gospel of *grace*. Two parables of Jesus underline this: the under-appreciated story of the two brothers (Matt. 21.28–32) and the magnificent parable of the labourers in the vineyard (Matt. 20.1–16), which is as glorious an announcement of grace as is to be found in the Bible.

We can achieve only a rudimentary survey of the topic of 'spiritual pain' in this chapter. A final category revolves around a set of familiar questions: 'Why me?' or 'Why her?' The theologian takes his life in his hands venturing into territory such as this. Structurally, we might say that the question falls into two parts: a general question and a specific question. The general question is, 'Why does anyone die?' The specific question is, 'Why is this person dying?'

The general question – why death? – brings us back to topics treated in Chapter 2. There are many approaches to an answer.

Some stress sin, saying that death was never part of God's intention;[11] others answer that dying is part of what it means to be a creature. Some synthesis of these approaches may be possible, in the idea that the human being is naturally mortal but that there is something about the *way* in which we are now mortal that is coloured, and rendered worse, by human rebellion.

We explore here the idea that death is part of what it means to be a creature. On this account, death is part of what it means for us to be finite: what it means for us not to be God, to be in time and not in eternity, to live in a world characterized by change, growth and decline. As Augustine of Hippo put it, the beauty of the ages is woven by things following one another, and therefore passing.[12] Dying comes along with being born; the possibility of birth is woven with the inevitability of death. Certainly, from the perspective of biology, the evolutionary advent of death seems to be tied up with the advent of sexual reproduction. Moreover, grief and love are bound together. The only way to be immune to the effects of death would be to love no one and nothing, but that would be to live in hell on earth. 'Grief is the price we pay for love,' remarked Queen Elizabeth II in her response to the attacks of 9/11.

As Edward Schillebeeckx put it, 'Death proves that man [and woman], at least corporeally, is a piece of nature, bound up with the transitoriness of the material world. Seen in this light, death is the clearest manifestation of the limitedness of the human condition.'[13] We are part of nature. Even the longest living trees die: bristlecone pines and giant sequoia. If we were exempt from death, we would not be part of nature.

Admittedly, the angels do not die, but they are not material and not in the flow of time in the same way as we are. They are angels; we are human beings. With materiality comes change, and with change comes death. However, with materiality much else also

---

11 They might cite Wisdom 1.13 and 2.24 – if those are authoritative books in their tradition – as justification.

12 *Literal Commentary on Genesis* I.viii.14.

13 'The Death of a Christian' in *The Layman in the Church, and other Essays* (New York: Alba House, 1963), p. 62.

comes: not only having parents, grandparents and godparents, and children, grandchildren and godchildren (most of us), but also living in time and therefore experiencing the world as a story, knowing surprise and novelty, being able to venture something, and hearing one note die away so that another can take its place.[14]

The other question, the specific question – why is *he*, why is *she* going to die? – is no more susceptible to a clear-cut answer than is the general question, indeed less so. Even on a scientific basis, it is often difficult to answer such *why* questions, to say exactly what led to this situation turning out the way it has. The theologian may be able to give some philosophical perspectives, which may or may not hold much usefulness, practically and pastorally speaking.

One response to the question 'Why *this person*?' is to invoke chance. The world unfolds with an element of chance, and sometimes this has terrible consequences. On the one hand, without chance there could be no novelty, no newness to life, nothing of the unexpected. On the other, this gene mutated, or that person was born with a particular, deleterious genetic make-up, and because of this, she is dying.

The question 'Why me?' or 'Why him?' is often expressed in a different way: 'Why is God not stepping in?' We ask, in other words, why there is no miracle. Most Christians believe in miracles, but miracles cannot be the norm. If *chance* is a partial philosophical reply to 'Why him?', then *order* is the partial philosophical reply to 'Why is there no miracle?' God gives laws and an order to the universe and does not change them as a rule. Looked at from another perspective, even a miracle would only be temporary. We are all going to die, eventually. As we will see in Chapter 8, in relation to the sacrament of anointing, the ultimate aim of that sacrament, even as a sacrament of healing, is salvation. It is natural to pray for healing and for a miracle, but

---

14 Moreover, those theologians who have broached the tricky topic as to whether the fallen angels can repent – and the answer is almost always that they cannot – have tended to link their doom to their immateriality. If our material experience of time and change is necessarily also one of death, then it is also one in which repentance is possible.

it is more necessary, ultimately, that we live and die within the salvation offered to us by God.

To venture any such thoughts is to be involved in the task of theodicy: of justifying the ways of God in the face of suffering. That is a perilous business, and in recent years the very idea of theodicy has come in for considerable criticism, from at least two perspectives. The first is that there is something potentially arrogant about human beings defending God, and a risk that we fail to see that God's ways are not our ways (Isa. 55.8).[15] The other is that a certain sort of explanation of suffering is pastorally insensitive at best, and immoral at worst. The betrayal would be an account of theodicy that explained evil to the extent of explaining it away. This is a theological own goal. Parents facing the loss of a child do not need to be told, 'It's all right, really,' or 'Looked at properly, it's all part of a good overall plan.'[16]

All this means that the best response to evil and suffering is rarely a theoretical or speculative one; it is a practical one. We might be able to offer some fragment of a thought in response to suffering; we might not. What we can do is contribute to the sort of holistic care explored in this book, for the dying and for their families and friends. We might say that we are in good company here, since God's response to evil and suffering was not theoretical and speculative; it was very practical: it was the incarnation, death and resurrection of his Son.

---

15 A good example of this criticism of certain sorts of theodicy is found in Brian Davies' book *The Reality of God and the Problem of Evil* (London: Continuum, 2006).

16 A particularly brilliant discussion of this comes from Rowan Williams in his essay 'Redeeming Sorrows: Marilyn McCord Adams and the Defeat of Evil', published in Mike Higton (ed.), *Wrestling with Angels* (London: SPCK, 2007), pp. 255–74.

6

Communication: Relating to Dying Patients and their Families

Communication lies at the heart of much that is important in ministry. In this chapter we consider the role of communication in ministry to the dying and their families and friends.

Visitors to the dying are quite often anxious about what to say to a dying person. There can be an entirely reasonable fear that we will say 'the wrong thing' and in so doing add to someone's burden, rather than bringing relief. The reality, however, is that most people who are dying want to be treated as 'normal', even if that means the occasional blunder. In the last analysis, avoiding conversation can, in fact, be motivated more by a wish to protect ourselves than a wish to protect the patient. We can take encouragement from Mother Teresa of Calcutta, who wrote that she 'would rather make mistakes in kindness and compassion than work miracles in unkindness and hardness'.[1] If we proceed on the basis of love and compassion, we cannot go far wrong. If we make loving others the central motivation, then we will find the words to say. In any case, as we discuss below, *how we are* in the company of a dying person is just as important, if not more, than *what we say*. This is the central message of this chapter. We look at this in terms of the topics that arise in these situations. More than that, we want to suggest the sort of 'trajectory' we might expect of such a conversation. We will cover listening, witnessing, questioning, clarification of understanding and closing.[2]

---

1 Mother Teresa, *A Gift for God: Prayers and Meditations* (San Francisco: Harper, 1996), p. 34.

2 This model draws on experience and concepts proposed by Roger Neighbour in *The Inner Consultation* (Lancaster: Radcliffe Publishing, 2005) and *The*

Listening

Dietrich Bonhoeffer, a twentieth-century pastor, theologian and martyr, wrote that 'the beginning of love for the brethren [as he put it] is learning to listen to them'.[3] The value of listening in pastoral work is widely acknowledged.[4] Dame Cicely Saunders talked about creating a 'climate of listening'.[5] When someone is in such an environment, she wrote, he or she will 'say things he [or she] wouldn't have said before'. Most people will be happy to talk if they feel that they are truly being met by a listening ear. Much of this depends upon a sense that the person listening is doing so with integrity. Trust is a foundation for communication, and while this is sometimes easier to spot than to describe, we can start by coming as ourselves, being open and honest. Relaxed body language and a smile are also likely to get us off to a good start.

Some people are 'natural listeners' but listening, all the same, is a skill, and it can be learned. For most of us, good listening requires that we take a conscious decision to do it properly. The more we practise attentive and pastorally sensitive listening, the more natural it will become. It is by no means a quality only possessed by professionals.

Silence has an important part to play. In our noisy, word-filled lives, silence can feel alien and uncomfortable. This can be felt most acutely when we are silent in the presence of another person. That is often described as an 'awkward' silence. Be that as it may, there is generally not enough silence in the world and in a pastoral situation silence is sometimes what is most needed: our presence

---

Inner Apprentice (Lancaster: Radcliffe Publishing, 2004). It also draws on the 'Calgary-Cambridge' method of communication skills, as laid out by Jonathan Silverman, Suzanne M. Kurtz and Juliet Draper in *Skills for Communicating with Patients*, 2nd edn (Lancaster: Radcliffe Publishing, 2005).

3 Dietrich Bonhoeffer, *Life Together* (New York: Harper & Row, 1954), p. 97.

4 On this subject, Anne Long's book *Listening* (London: Darton, Longman & Todd, 1990) is perceptive on the multi-dimensional nature of listening.

5 Quoted in Long, *Listening*, p. 39.

without words. The simple knowledge that you are there – that you want to be there and you came to visit – can be immensely powerful. Sitting alongside a dying patient, and expressing solidarity with his or her suffering, is a profound act of human love. Significant peace, even a transformation of the immediate situation, can occur simply through this silent presence.

Listening, by its nature, requires silence on our part. People sometimes reflect on a time with a dying person, or their relatives, and say, 'I *just* listened', with a sense of inadequacy. However, just listening can be *just* what is needed. Likely as not, we can all recall times where we have felt better purely from the presence of another person who has cared enough to give his time to listen. One person's listening silence can give another person time to think and reflect, to ponder and respond.

A useful idea here is *active* listening. This means treating listening as an action, rather than as something that happens automatically, simply by being present in the same room. It means being fully focused on that person alone and using more than just our ears. Active listening more or less requires that all parties are sitting comfortably. If someone is in pain or feeling sick, that should be addressed first, if that is at all possible. Facing emotional distress is much more difficult when someone is in physical discomfort.

Fatigue is common among terminally ill people and should be taken into consideration in deciding when to visit and how long to stay. Regular, short conversations may be more appropriate than an hour of in-depth conversation. As far as possible, we should ensure that the environment is quiet, so that the parties can hear one another easily. Some people may use hearing aids. If so, make sure that these are fitted well and working properly before the conversation starts. The subject matter may well have 'private' elements, which means that the setting should be appropriate. It should be somewhere where each person feels comfortable to talk freely. In a hospital, this may involve asking the ward staff for use of a separate room.

If there is a time constraint, it is important to mention at the beginning of the conversation that you need to leave at a particular time, adding that, for the time you are with this person, you are entirely committed to them. Making this comment up front avoids any awkward clock-watching or having to close the conversation abruptly.

Research has suggested that between 60 and 70 per cent of meaning in an exchange is derived from non-verbal behaviour.[6] An open body posture is best, and good eye contact will underline that you are committed to the person you are visiting, and that you have time for them. If the person's first language differs from yours, it may be wise to request a translator. Most palliative care services will have access to a bank of local translators. Arrange a mutually convenient time for the meeting between the three (or more) of you. When speaking using a translator, it is important to keep the patient still as the focus. Eye contact will again help here.

Bearing witness

A crucially important dimension of work with the dying is what we have called 'bearing witness', although it could also have the more prosaic title of 'taking note'. The point is to show that what is said has been received by another person, and to bear witness to the sense that what is shared is something that matters.

People naturally desire to be witnessed, to be taken account of, not least when they are in distress. It is almost a truism that we usually feel better simply for having voiced our concerns. This is certainly borne out in the setting of palliative care.

Witnessing another person's distress is demanding. It is the work of a servant, where attitude takes priority over skills. We will probably need to empty ourselves of our own needs, expectations and desires in order to be fully present. This is time for the sick person. She may otherwise have been cast very much in the role of the passive listener by the medical process, with doctors and others doing the talking and passing on information. That

---

6 Isa N. Engleberg and Dianna Wynn, *Working in Groups: Communication Principles and Strategies* (Boston, MA: Houghton Mifflin, 2000), p. 133.

dynamic begins with the initial diagnosis and continues with the discussion of treatment plans and instructions as to how to take particular medication. Most people in that situation are consequently yearning for an opportunity to talk rather than listen yet again.[7] In a medical setting such as a hospital, the chaplain or member of the chaplaincy team may be the only person able to offer this sort of precious time to listen and to witness. Clergy and other visitors can do the same.

We make most progress here, and the transaction is most valuable, if it is undergirded by the sense of trust that we have already mentioned. Most people will assume this trust in conversations with clergy and, if so, conversations may go deep very quickly. Physicians recount similar stories, of 'strangers' walking off the street into a surgery and, because of the doctor's position, being happy to talk about very personal matters at a first meeting. This is an enormous privilege and one never to be abused. This said, the prime value of what is going on is of one person sitting with another in their distress, simply as two human beings, and the question of role or status is ultimately immaterial.

In this act of bearing witness, our purpose is to listen, share and hold another person in our thoughts and attention. We may not be able to reverse or resolve what is discussed, but we can hear it and *witness* it. In so doing, we show a certain validation and respect for the humanity of the other person: the very humanity that makes suffering so awful.

Questioning

The purpose of asking questions is to gather information in order to help us to understand the emotional pain being experienced. If the one who is ministering is closed off and uninterested, there is little hope of that 'witnessing' we have just mentioned. Lack of

---

7 As an aspect of this, we can note a recent interest in patients' narratives. In many hospices, patients have been given the opportunity to write down their thoughts and feelings. Sometimes this takes the form of a chronological life story, but it can be expressed in poetry or art.

communication can place a dying person in a situation of profound, and profoundly unhelpful, emotional isolation.

Many questions will arise naturally from the listening and witnessing process. It will be clear what is obvious to ask and explore. It may, however, be useful to think about a conversation as traversing a number of levels: the deeper the level, the more hidden is the emotion that belongs to it; the deeper the level, the more difficult it is to express and explore.

We might consider the following model:

Levels of conversation
External environment/outside world
Knowledge
Thoughts and feelings
Hopes and desires
Meaning

If we are stuck for words, it is easiest to start at the top layer. This is why we so often turn to the weather in opening a conversation with a complete stranger. This is not without its own logic: it would not be appropriate, or comfortable, to ask someone we do not know well what meaning they attribute to their lives as an opening gambit (although we might all know Christians who take this approach). These potentially trivial opening topics help to build a rapport. We might just as well notice and talk about something in the immediate environment, such as flowers on a bedside table, the book someone is reading, or the photograph in the lounge. The questions that follow, for the most part, should be 'open questions', which is to say, ones with no assumptions made as to the answers. Questions that could be answered with a simple 'yes' or 'no' are best avoided. Open questions, such as 'How are you?', 'How are you finding things?', 'What do you think about x?', 'How does that make you feel?' or 'What would you like to do about x?', provoke an exploration, in contrast to closed questions such as 'Don't you think that you should *x*?' or 'I presume you are going to?'

As another rule, it is best never to assume that *you* know what the *sick person* knows, thinks or feels. The process of information gathering should start from what they reveal, not what is assumed. It is tempting, especially when time is short, to make bold, presumptive statements to get the conversation going, but that is not a good way to develop a relationship. It also risks, on occasions, going seriously askew. Ideally, we will be able to follow cues provided by the patient and respond to the points that she raises, with the aim of seeking to understand. As rapport is cemented and trust is gained, it will be easier to ask deeper questions, touching on perspectives and feelings, hopes and desires.

At the core of communication with a dying person is the question of whether we should aim to encourage the individual to 'face his illness' or the reality of her situation. No single answer can be given. Much depends on the individual. In general, gentleness must be the key to any approach. No conversation will benefit from being forced. Beyond that, we should ask ourselves *why* we want to probe deeper and *why* we want the truth exposed. We all have an innate desire for the truth to be acknowledged and shared, and it is difficult to collude or be dishonest with someone who has our trust. All the same, the motive for questioning must always come back to what is best for the individual in front of us. There is no value in pushing someone beyond his or her limits. The pace of a conversation should be set by the patient and not by the questioner. If it is clear that the patient is blocking deeper discussion, then do not force the conversation. It may be that on a subsequent visit, once trust has developed and time has passed, the discussion will go deeper, pressing on towards the reality of the situation and thus towards acceptance. Even those who prefer 'other things' as the topic of conversation usually come round, by a circuitous route, to talking about their illness once trust is established. However, if a person remains in denial, it can be very difficult to proceed further than the first or second layer of conversation.

People differ over how much they want to know and want to share about their condition. There is rarely harm in asking someone what kind of person he is: does he like to speak frankly about what is happening? What would he find it helpful to speak about on this visit? Asking the question helps to avoid awkward blunders early in a conversation. It also suggests a respect for the person as an individual, which in turn can lead to trust.

Relatives will occasionally suggest that the truth should be withheld from an ill spouse or parent, usually as it relates to prognosis and the terminal nature of the illness. In most cases this request is made out of love and a desire to protect a loved one. It would be very easy to collude wholeheartedly with this, but in reality it can lead to a web of complicated lies. This is more a question for medics than for church visitors, but if it does arise, a helpful response can be to say that you will agree not to bring up the issue at hand intentionally; if, however, the patient asks you directly, then you will be honest. One of the main principles of medical ethics is respecting the autonomy of the patient. Part of this is the individual's right to know the truth of his situation. People hardly ever ask these questions unless they want to know the truth. In all of this, the process of facing reality must be clothed with love, sincerity and compassion.

Clarification of understanding

An important element or stage of communication is stopping to check understanding. Once you feel you have a sense of what someone is expressing, try to summarize it, using language appropriate to the person involved. We might, for example, start with such phrases as 'Can I just check that I have understood what you are saying / how you are feeling / what is upsetting you?', followed by a summary. If something remains unclear then, if it is appropriate, ask for clarification. Again it is easy to assume understanding and then to misrepresent the real issue. Sometimes, several visits, or the elapse of some considerable time, may be necessary before full understanding is achieved.

Closing

The way we close an encounter is as important as how we begin it or conduct the bulk of it. Before leaving it is imperative to check how a patient is. Dr Hanratty was a former Medical Director of St Joseph's Hospice in London. His advice to doctors was that they should 'glance back' at the patient after leaving the bedside, which demonstrates a wonderful sensitivity. We can all learn from this example. He wrote:

> After talking to a patient, a glance back after leaving the bedside is most instructive, as the patient's facial expression at that moment gives an uninhibited indication of the emotional state. A worried, frightened, anxious expression necessitates a return to the bedside as a patient in that state should not be left alone.[8]

We should aim to leave well. Ideally, having listened, witnessed, questioned and clarified the concerns, some response is called for. This may be to plan another visit or to request consent to ask another colleague or a member of the palliative care team to visit, to help with the emotional problems elicited. If the person was previously unknown to you, then leaving contact details may be an opening to further discussions, in case he wishes to speak more. Some people find a holding cross or a prayer card a helpful emotional support. Giving a gift such as this marks the transition of a departure. Touch can also be a very powerful communicator. Squeezing a person's hand before leaving or a gentle touch on the arm may bear witness to a shared experience, to compassion and a respect of what has just been said. That said, touch should be used selectively and appropriately: it can be considered invasive, and for some ministers and visitors this means of communication does not come naturally.

---

8 J. F. Hanratty, 'Care of the Dying' in *Philosophy of Terminal Illness* (Hackney: St Joseph's Hospice, 1987).

Challenges to communication

Communication can be impeded or compromised for a variety of reasons. A patient may, for instance, have impaired senses. We have mentioned the importance of checking if a patient wears a hearing aid and, if so, of checking that it works before embarking on a conversation. When talking to someone with visual loss, cues from other senses may be heightened, such as the sound of shuffling or rustling papers. Introduction of your role is also likely to take longer without visual cues. In this situation, some people will naturally reach out their hand to find yours. Touch can help to make a connection and contributes to a sense of trust. As we have just noted, touch is not for all patients and not for all visitors. However, it may aid communication in this situation.

Some patients are unable to speak because of their illness, or at least to speak easily. They may have had a stroke, which has slurred their speech, or be suffering from a brain tumour that affects the speech area of the brain, making it difficult for them to find words. Sioned remembers a patient who could not speak because of a brain tumour, but he could sing. The music therapist worked with him so that he could sing his requests, which was both fascinating and humbling.

Some patients have difficulty speaking because they have a tracheostomy: an opening directly into the trachea (breathing tube) which sits just below the voice box, usually to bypass an obstruction and aid breathing. Speaking is difficult because air no longer passes over the vocal cords. Sound can be made if the patient presses fingers over the opening to the tracheostomy, but this can be exhausting for them, and it also carries some risk of infection. Some patients will have a 'speaking valve', which is inserted in the tracheostomy tube and allows for clearer speech. Again, using this can be very tiring and often frustrating for the patient. Patience is required from the listener, and ideally a quiet environment, as often speech may amount to no more than a whisper.

Also very frustrating for some is the loss of the ability to speak because of damage to nerves or muscles controlling the voice box, for example in patients with motor neurone disease (or ALS). They may be able to write instead, if they have retained the use of their arms, and some will choose an electronic device such as a 'light-writer'. This allows text to be typed and then a voice reproduces the words. This can reopen the ability to communicate, although the conversations that follow will likely be slow. Again patience and compassion, even resilience, are required from the listener.

A patient without a voice

Sioned remembers a very challenging and humbling conversation with a patient with MND who used a light-writer. He was a delightful man in his mid-seventies whose disease had affected his ability to speak. On top of this, the disease had affected his facial muscles, so it was very difficult really to know what he was thinking or feeling. During his admission to the hospice, she would pop in on her ward round and see how he was. Sitting down beside him, she would ask him how he was and he would type 'OK', nothing more. After several days of nothing more than 'OK', he decided to write more and she was unprepared for what he wrote: 'How long have I got to live?' These questions are challenging to answer at the best of times, but faced with someone whose facial expressions she could not read, and who could not speak back, this was very challenging indeed. She knew that this was a precious moment and, as she always did in these situations, she sent up an 'arrow' prayer for guidance in this conversation, and for them not to be interrupted. She knew that this question had taken a great deal of courage to ask. He had made himself very vulnerable and she did not want to waste this opportunity. As previously mentioned, honesty and integrity are hallmarks of palliative care. If a person asks, then it is our duty to respond. So she sat with him and touched his arm and checked that he wanted to talk about this here and now, not to wait until his wife came. He was able to nod: he wanted to pursue this. She asked him how long *he* felt he had, remembering that it is never right to assume what another knows. She waited until he typed. He typed, 'Not long'.

She was keen to maintain eye contact with him, and not make the machine the focus of their conversation. She nodded back gently in agreement. She asked him if that was a shock to him and waited anxiously as he typed, letter by letter, 'No, I am ready. I have had enough.' She reassured him that as he got weaker, they would do everything they could to make him comfortable. He simply typed, 'Thank you' and touched her hand. He had no further questions. She just sat with him for a while, wanting him to know that she had witnessed him and treasured his vulnerability.

Not every encounter is quite so profound. Sioned also remembers another patient who used his light-writer to tell jokes, not all of them suitable for the consultant's ward round, but very funny!

Relating to the dying patient and their families: the fruits of the Spirit

Ministry with the dying involves a commitment to *being with* them, of presence and accompaniment, as we have said. For those involved in this work for the first time, one of the most significant concerns is the worry that they will say something stupid or unhelpful, and make an already difficult situation worse. Concern such as this represents a genuine attitude of care and humility. In this second half of this chapter, we consider a model for being with a dying person based on the 'fruits of the Spirit' listed by Paul in Galatians 5.22–23: 'the fruit of the Spirit is love, joy, peace, forbearance, kindness, goodness, faithfulness, gentleness and self-control. Against such things there is no law.'

We find reassurance here that those who minister to the dying are not alone in these difficult situations. It is not all 'down to us'; the Holy Spirit is alongside us. As we enter the room of a dying patient, or sit in the lounge of a tearful relative, we can remember that we need seek no more than to co-operate with God, and to be someone through whom his presence may be seen and felt. We will look at each of the fruits individually, to give some practical pointers.

Love is the fundamental character of the approach we will

want to take. Our motives must be to do the best we can for the person we are with. The fruit of love is the one from which all others grow, and is the principle from which all of our care must proceed. If we come without love for the other person, the other fruits will struggle to be seen.

We are to come alongside those who are suffering not from a position of power or authority but as equals. We come to share in their human suffering as fellow human beings, as Jesus shared in others' sufferings, and as he himself suffered. Introduce yourself, therefore, as a person rather than as a title.

As Paul also wrote in Galatians, our task is to share someone's load (6.2). Just sitting alongside someone can be immensely supportive. The simple presence of a comforter can bring healing. It is not always necessary to find the right words; just sitting, and by that showing solidarity, may be all that some people need.

Turning to the next fruit, it may seem wrong or disrespectful to consider being *joyful* in such circumstances. However, the joy that comes from God is not inappropriate. It is a joy that stems from our hope in Christ and from the knowledge of Christ's love, demonstrated in his death and resurrection. This joy can be shared explicitly when people ask; it can be demonstrated in our attitude and demeanour.

Joy exists alongside sorrow, and they are not mutually exclusive. Joy can bring relief from sadness, if only for a while. It is very difficult to remain in a situation of despair and sorrow indefinitely; a few minutes of cheer, even a moment, can mark a profound break from the depths of sadness. The best indication of this joy is not denial but peace.

Joy is most often associated with people, but it can also be communicated through the environment in which the patient or relatives find themselves. Photographs and flowers, for example, can transform a hospital room into a more joyous, less clinical place to be. Patients should be encouraged to surround themselves with people and items that bring them joy.

A distinctive feature of hospices is often the amount of laughter that can be heard in them. Against expectations, many people find hospices to be happy places. That can be a helpful observation to recall if we are talking to someone who is ill at home and perhaps feeling anxious about moving into a hospice. She may have an image in mind of a dark, dour and depressing environment, from which no one ever returns. In describing something different, we are only telling the truth.

Some patients enjoy being pampered: having a manicure, a hand massage, or a visit from the hairdresser, for instance. Music is also important for many people. Such treats are often available in a hospice and sometimes to relatives too; we can encourage relatives to find ways to take some time out of the demands of visiting in this way. Relatives often feel guilty about looking after themselves and feeling anything remotely like joy, and this is understandable. One useful role for a minister or other represent-ative of the Church can be to stress that caring for oneself, and being cared for, is important. Looking after someone who is dying is physically and emotionally draining. Stamina is required. The final days often arrive on the back of weeks or months of tireless, but tiring, caring. We owe it to the person who is being cared for, and to ourselves, to take some respite.

This seems an appropriate moment to talk about the use of humour. Much work has been done on humour and illness. The phrase 'laughter is the best medicine' may not be quite accurate but it is onto something. Research shows that we typically feel better for having laughed.[9] As is often the case, the main principle when it comes to humour is to be yourself. If you communicate easily and readily through humour, do so. That said, reading the situation is also important, asking yourself whether it is the right time and place for humour. We would do well to take some time to understand the people we are with: some may be natural jokers, while others prefer a more serious approach. A smile is even more generally applicable. As Mother Teresa put it, 'Let us always meet each other with a smile, for the smile is the beginning of love.'[10] A

9 Catherine M. Macdonald, 'A Chuckle a Day Keeps the Doctor Away: Therapeutic Humor and Laughter', *Journal of Psychosocial Nursing and Mental Health Services*, 42 (2004), pp. 18–25.

10 From her Nobel Peace Prize Lecture in 1979, quoted in *Nobel Lectures, Peace 1971–80* (Singapore: World Scientific Publishing Company, 1997).

smile breeds a smile, giving others the permission to smile back.

The places where people die can be very busy, whether that is a hospital ward or a home where carers, visitor and professionals are in frequent attendance. Creating an environment where *peace* can be experienced is therefore important. As we suggested in Chapter 5, imagine a time when you have had the flu and were laid up in bed. This is the closest we might come to feeling the fatigue often experienced at the end. Even the smallest tasks are exhausting and people need quiet time to rest and not be troubled by anyone or anything.

Again, when it comes to peace, the physical environment is important. In a hospital or hospice, a side room can be requested to provide some quiet. Most patients in nursing homes will have their own rooms, and at home, a room should be created that is not shared for any other purpose: Grandad's bed should not be in the lounge where everyone comes in to watch the television. A space where peace can be had must be available.

Professionals tend to see patients during working hours, so outside of this period patients are often available for more peaceful encounters. It can be that the 'deeper' conversations come about in the quiet of the night, when only the night staff are on duty.

Silence can be a wonderful thing. As we mentioned previously, caring for a dying person or relative is not about 'saying the right thing' with profound, meaningful words. Remember that the use of silence and touch can be powerful means of communication.

As a visitor, try to bring peace with you. Preparation is the key here. Gather as much information as you can, or is necessary, from other professionals and carers involved with the patient and family before visiting. If you know what has gone before and what you may encounter, this will help with any nerves or anxiety you have. Pray before arriving that you will be filled with peace. Patients and relatives will experience that peace, and benefit from it a great deal. However much of a rush we may be in, try to enter with a measured pace, and not out of breath. Amid the hustle and bustle, your visit may be a haven of peace.

This brings us to *forbearance*. Give yourself the space to spend 'quality time' with dying patients and their relatives. Some visits, of course, may need to be short, and this cannot always be pre-dicted. But if your time is restricted, then communicate early on in the discussion how long you have available. You can always offer to visit again, to continue the conversation.

Some situations can really test a visitor's patience: perhaps a patient or relative is hard of hearing and requires us to repeat our sentences; or we are in a noisy hospital ward where we cannot hear the person speak while an important conversation is unfold-ing. We might be with a patient who is restless and agitated, or come across an angry relative and be the one at the receiving end of their upset. This is where having time to give can be invalu-able. You may find yourself being the only person who is able to devote the time that makes all the difference. Remaining through the difficulty, if you can, speaks volumes.

Some people's stories require forbearance. Even seasoned hos-pice and hospital chaplains, with years of experience, can find themselves in new situations and facing unexpected heartaches. This may involve listening to a story full of repeated losses, or of a deep sense of unfairness in a person's life, or being with some-one wanting to discuss a setback to their faith. In the words of Reinhold Niebuhr, in situations such as this we need 'the serenity to accept the things I cannot change, the courage to change the things I can, and the wisdom to know the difference'.

Sometimes it is easy to see how things could be improved. We may be able to help a sick person who is hard of hearing simply by asking a member of the nursing staff for access to a quieter room. If a patient is restless because she is in pain or feeling sick, we can alert a member of the medical team to see whether an assess-ment could help. On the other hand, things are often beyond our control, and factors cannot be changed: the young mother who is dying; the teenager with Down's syndrome who is losing her dear father but no one is quite sure how much she understands; the elderly woman whose approaching death has brought long-held grief to the surface for her baby son she lost 60 years before. Faced with these difficult stories, while we might wonder whether there is anything that we can do to change this situation, in a sense, there always is: simply being with someone. This 'ministry of presence' makes the situation different from how it would be without someone there. When we pray for the fruit of forbearance, we can not only trust the person and the situation to God, but also commit ourselves to being whatever sign we can of his presence and care.[11]

Jesus taught us to love one another as he himself loved us. One of the main principles of care – the fruit of *kindness* – is to treat others as you would want to be treated if you were dying yourself. We might also think of how we would want our husband, parent, sister or children to be cared for if we were dying, and treat other people's relatives in that way too.

Kindness is the motive to do our best for another person. It will be expressed in different ways depending on the circumstances. A key here is knowing what the patient wants, as far as is possible. For that, we – or more likely the family and the medical team – must engage in dialogue to obtain a deeper understanding of what is important to the person who is sick.

On occasion, being kind may involve challenging what the patient believes is best for him, especially if that helps him to explore 'kinder' options. For example, a patient might be determined to die at home but then refuse to have carers other than his elderly wife, who is clearly struggling. If the wife confides in you that she is exhausted, but does not want to deny her husband his desire to die at home, the kinder option is probably not to stay quiet but rather – if it falls within the parameters of your relationship and ministry – gently to challenge the status quo. You could highlight your concerns to a health professional involved in care. If you know the couple well, you may have the opportunity to talk through with them what is working and what is not, and open up the conversation for consideration of other, *kinder* options.

God's *goodness* is present in many ways: in nature, in music, in touch and a smile, to name just a few. The concept of 'reframing', which we have already encountered, involves looking at a

---

11 The British theologian Sam Wells has written with great insight about 'being with', for instance in his book with Marcia Owen, *Living Without Enemies: Being Present in the Midst of Violence* (Downers Grove, IL: IVP, 2011).

bad situation and being able to see what in it is positive. Reframing is very different from denial: it is seeing the good that exists despite the suffering, rather than denying the suffering. Goodness is everywhere but sometimes it can seem deeply hidden. Obviously, it will frequently seem that way to dying people and their relatives. Our task may be to help someone to articulate gratitude for what has been good, and to foster awareness of the 'little things' that remain.

We need to meet people where they are and to be sensitive to their circumstances. Patients or relatives may feel annoyed if, amid their anger, they are told how beautiful the weather is outside or how good the flowers are looking in their garden. But given time, we might hope that something can be recognized as good and positive: something that is present or has come out of the situation in which they find themselves. In all of this, goodness is also found in being humble, respectful and polite. There is no goodness in arrogance and rudeness. It is an honour to be invited into the life of a dying person and we should mark it as such.

'What is it that helps you when life gets difficult?' You may already have a sense of the person's answer to this question, if the patient or relative is known to you well. It can be a useful opening gambit in speaking to those who are less familiar, and a way into articulating where they put their *faith*.

It will be clear to most people where *your* own faith lies, perhaps because of clerical clothing or a badge that says 'chaplaincy visitor'. Whether chaplains should wear clerical collars is a matter of considerable debate. For some patients it will be reassuring, demonstrating clearly who you are and what you represent. For others it can be a barrier. Ultimately, being with people is more important than what you wear. Equally, being faithful to one's tradition in this matter is part of showing integrity.

We can offer to pray with patients and relatives with a Christian faith, and it is useful to have a book of appropriate prayers to hand for this, and be familiar with scriptural verses that usually bring comfort.[12] Some clergy carry pocket-sized prayer cards to

---

12 Different churches produce their own books of resources, alongside those offered more widely by publishing houses. For the Church of England there

give to patients. Patients can gain enormous comfort from a holding cross, especially people who may be too weak to engage in prayer. Some hospices and hospitals hold services of Communion in a chapel, which patients, relatives and staff can attend. Communion can also be brought to the bedside if the patient is too weak to move. Patients may want to be anointed with oil, but this may require an explanation beforehand. Seek the relative's consent if the patient is unconscious.[13]

In the face of death, people may want to ask the deepest of faith-related questions, and view you as a person they can ask about such matters. Others may be less direct but still searching, and a gentle offer to speak about faith may be accepted. Never make assumptions that a Christian with faith must therefore be coping well. Illness invites the possibility of questioning and can rock previously held beliefs; some patients will have lost their Christian faith. Patients who have never believed may fear that 'the vicar' will try to convert them on their deathbed, and give him a wide berth. Clergy may also be seen as a walking sign of impending death, almost like the grim reaper. In that case, if they speak at all, they are only likely to make progress in building a relationship if they demonstrate a willingness to listen and a reluctance to judge; from this a valuable conversation may emerge.

Most hospice and hospital chaplains will be able to contact religious leaders of other faiths. If we are visiting the dying frequently, or have a wide-ranging role in such a setting, it can be useful to have a working knowledge of beliefs and practices from other religions, especially with regard to death and dying.

Ultimately, faithfulness comes in the form of reliability: if we turn up when we promise to come and do what we promise to do. With this in mind, we can turn to the next fruit, *gentleness*, which can be seen in how we are with others. Gentleness allows us to be with others without fear and without the presence of an

---

is *Common Worship: Pastoral Ministry Companion* (London: Church House Publishing, 2012), alongside which we might want to add a book of more devotional prayers, for instance *Lift Up Your Hearts* (London: SPCK, 2010).

13 On the final sacraments, of confession, anointing and Communion, see Andrew Davison, *Why Sacraments?* (London: SPCK, 2013).

overbearing ego. There is no struggle for power or domination in gentleness. We exhibit it when we have nothing to prove about ourselves. Again, this shows how relating to the dying person and their families is so much more than finding the right words to say. A gentle approach will speak volumes. A gentle smile, touch, pace of speech, volume of voice, appropriate language, eye contact and obvious willingness to listen are warming to those in need of comfort.

The ministry of caring for the dying can be difficult and emotionally draining. Looking after yourself is therefore paramount, as we discussed in Chapter 4. Some points are reiterated here since they bear directly on *self-control*.

Clergy and lay ministers are usually in charge of their own timetable, although it is likely to be both busy and changeable. If you know that you are going to see someone who is dying, think carefully about what you schedule on either side of the visit. Give yourself time for preparation beforehand, time to pray and gather your thoughts, and time afterwards, to pray and reflect. Put some space between the visit and what comes next: time to go for a walk, for instance. Do this even if that next 'task' is going home to everyday life at its most normal. Know how much time you have to give the visit and stick to it if possible. Self-control is also important in encounters with patients and carers. Be ready to admit when you do not know the answer to a question, or when there are no easy answers. In this way we share in the uncertainty and the struggle.

A particular concern frequently raised by those preparing for ministry to the dying is whether to show emotion in front of patients and families. In general, there is certainly no shame in doing so, and it reinforces a sense of our equality as human beings. Doctors sometimes cry with patients and families in response to what needs to be said, or from seeing the suffering of others. However, in order to minister to others, we need to know when to use an element of self-control. Sometimes it is wrong to fight tears; on other occasions it falls to us to be the one who 'carries' a situation, and therefore to 'be strong'. The share we have in the pain and suffering of others should not shift, at least too far, into a position where roles are reversed, and grieving families are looking after the minister. A relationship is a two-way affair, but we need to have alternative relationships in which to share any burdens we have, rather than placing them on patients and carers.

Self-awareness is needed for us to recognize whether the emotions we experience might stem from unresolved personal grief. Doctors are not good at subjecting themselves to regular supervision, often seeing it as surplus to requirements, and clergy are rarely much better. Hospital and hospice chaplains, however, will often say that supervision should be considered necessary, in order to reflect on such dynamics helpfully. Supervision provides a setting in which we can recount the pastoral encounters we have found difficult and examine our own emotional responses to them.

We propose that Paul's lists of the gifts of the Holy Spirit can usefully form the template for the way in which we seek to relate to, and minister to, those who are dying. They are the Spirit's work, gifts given so that they might become the foundation for our work. This is a work that the Spirit does in and through us, but which is nevertheless our own. The fruits are characteristics for us to seek in each individual encounter, and to pray for regularly. We wish to grow into these characteristics over the course of a lifetime, such that we can be channels of God's grace by being ourselves.

7

Terminal Care

Care in the last days of life is known as terminal care. This can be a precious time; as C. S. Lewis put it, 'It is incredible how much happiness, even how much gaiety, we sometimes had together after all hope of recovery was gone. How long, how tranquilly, how nourishingly, we talked together that last night!'[1] Time itself is brought into sharp focus in these days and the imminence of separation becomes a stark reality. This is a period where the holistic care of the patient and their loved ones is paramount, along with co-ordinated teamwork. Done well, the care provided in these last days can have a powerful effect on all those involved. Done badly, it can promote fear and regrets, provoke ruminating questions and ultimately lead to a much more complex reaction of grief.

Diagnosing dying

Dying is a natural and unavoidable process. The cause of death will, of course, vary, and on this account so will the duration of the dying process. For the purposes of this book, we are looking at expected death, rather than sudden or accidental death.

Even when we are certain that a person will die from her illness, it can be hard to discern when someone is entering the last few days of life. The task of 'diagnosing dying' is by no means an exact science. Sometimes, patients themselves will tell us that they are dying. Sioned can distinctively remember a man telling

---

1 *A Grief Observed* (London: Faber and Faber, 1961), p. 14.

her that he was going to die in two days' time. She thought, rather confidently, that he looked far too well for this to be the case. However, he was right. That evening he deteriorated significantly and, sure enough, he died on the day he said he would. Staff may also have an intuitive sense when someone is dying. Doctors soon learn to pay attention when certain nurses speak on this matter. There is an old wives' tale that 'people get better to die', and people do sometimes become more alert and animated for a short period before their final decline. Good memories can follow from the opportunities that this can allow.

Various things happen to our bodies when we are dying. In broad terms, the different systems that maintain life, such as the respiratory and cardiovascular systems, start to shut down. The normal functions performed by the organs in our body, such as providing energy and excreting waste, stop working properly. Eventually, the organs such as the liver, lungs and brain fail. The final loss is of the heartbeat. In this last phase, the patient will get weaker, and find it more difficult to get out of bed or even to sit up. A profound fatigue is likely to descend, to which the patient will gradually submit. Appetite recedes, although we may still feel thirst, for which sips of fluid will help. Once someone becomes less conscious, wetting the lips, tongue and inside of the mouth with a 'sponge on a stick' can be comforting. Taking medication by mouth becomes more difficult, so it is likely to be given by a different method, often by a syringe driver. The drugs inside the syringe will help with a variety of complaints including pain, nausea, anxiety and chest secretions. Doses are reviewed at least daily to check that they are providing the best possible comfort for the patient. As we noted in Chapter 5, if the dosages are not sufficient, then additional amounts known as 'breakthrough doses' can be given.

As the dying person becomes less conscious, there will be less control over bladder and bowel function. A catheter will commonly be fitted, which takes away the possibility of wetting the bed and provides dignity for the patient. This should be discussed with the patient first, if he is conscious and coherent enough. If not, then a discussion will be had with the family.

Patients start to look different, especially as the rate of deterioration accelerates. Generally, the complexion becomes paler and more drawn, producing a sunken effect. Once adequate dosages of medication have been established, patients may lose their frowns and look more peaceful. Some patients may become flushed, which can be a side-effect of the medication. They may also be sweaty and clammy, sometimes with a mottled appearance. Their hands and feet start to feel cold.

Breathing patterns also change. Breathing may become more rapid and is sometimes accompanied by a rattle, where the breathing is very 'chesty' and noisy. As we noted in Chapter 5, medication can be given via the syringe driver to help to dry these secretions, although it is not always effective. The sound can be distressing to witness and an explanation to the family and friends by a medical or nursing colleague is helpful.

In comatose patients, we characteristically encounter what is called a Cheyne-Stokes breathing pattern. This alternates between deep, rapid breaths and a period of not breathing at all for 10 to 20 seconds. It can be terribly disconcerting for family and friends sitting by the patient: the interval before the patient breathes again can seem like an eternity. Reassurance that this is 'normal' can help.

The breathing pattern usually changes noticeably just prior to death. There will either be a period of 'gasping' breaths or a series of very rapid breaths followed by a few long, deep breaths. Occasionally, a last involuntary breath will occur after you think that breathing has ceased. A doctor or nurse might wait for up to a minute after the last breath before confirming someone has died, to ensure that no more breaths will be taken.

Delirium or confusion can occur as someone dies. This can be distressing for the family to witness. Part of providing dignity in care is to give an appropriate level of medication, usually via a syringe driver, to help restore their peace.

Emotionally, we start to withdraw as we die, and this forms part of the separation process. There will be less communication and touch as energy levels and consciousness diminish. The sense of hearing is said to be the last sense to go and some responses can be observed in a semi-conscious or unconscious patient at the sound of a familiar voice. Doctors often encourage relatives to continue talking to their loved one, even in an unconscious state, as he may be able to hear and gain some comfort from familiar voices. This may be an opportunity for the family to say things they still want to say while the person is still alive, even if the patient is unable to respond.

Many anecdotes are told of remarkable spiritual encounters as people are dying, and we can both attest to this. These include visions of angels, or of loved ones who have died before, or hearing heavenly music playing; these can provide comfort and meaning. The truth is, we do not know what is going on in these situations. What some onlookers may label as odd or confused behaviour could be a highly significant experience. No one should deny that dying is a deeply spiritual matter.[2]

Although death is a certainty, the period of dying itself may be filled with uncertainty. The patient, friends and relatives may be anxious to know 'how long'. Doctors hold a more or less common mind that it serves no purpose to attempt to predict the day or the hour, as it is often wrong. All the same, some general indication can be helpful and a doctor will make a suggestion if it is possible. Most people are just looking for a benchmark by which they can prepare themselves and, if necessary, make plans. While some diseases have a comparatively clear trajectory, certain cancers being an example, others, such as end-stage heart failure or dementia, have a less predictable path. As a rough rule of thumb there is wisdom in the following observation: 'When we see someone deteriorating from week to week we are often talking in terms of weeks, when that deterioration is from day to day then we are usually talking in terms of days, but everyone is different.'[3]

---

2 The American socio-linguist Anne Bower has conducted extensive research in this area with those nurses and medical auxiliaries who spend the most time with patients at the time of death (but who are not the subject of studies as often as doctors are). Her forthcoming book *Others to the Margin Come* will recount common experiences related by the dying in their last hours and moments.

3 Max Watson, Caroline Lucas, Andrew Hoy and Jo Wells, *Oxford Handbook of Palliative Care* (Oxford: Oxford University Press, 2009), p. 929.

Even this trend can be bucked, however, and whatever the length of the dying phase, the emphasis will be on providing care and dignity throughout. Gaining a sense of this can be very reassuring, and regular communication and updates will prove invaluable.

One fundamental principle behind care of the dying is co-ordinated teamwork and good communication, among all those involved in the spiritual care of an individual. Ideally, a minister would be informed of an imminent death of a member of a congregation, as might someone who has been visiting in the role of a chaplain. Occasionally, we are called to be with people we have never met before, which is more challenging, but the same principles endure. Often there is shared care and good liaison between chaplains, parish priests and others. This is to be encouraged.

As a visitor you may find yourself present as the moment of death approaches. Check with the family to make sure they are happy for you to be there. Some may want to be alone with the patient at the time of death, but many families find the presence of a Christian representative reassuring.[4]

Witnessing the moment of death is a profound experience. It can provoke deep responses in onlookers, resonating with our own losses or potential losses. It can equally be a humbling experience, where love is expressed in abundance. Your role at this time is simply to be there; your presence will be a comfort and service. Do not pretend that you are not human. Shedding tears should not be interpreted as failure but as empathy.

We are likely to count it an honour to have been present at the time of someone's death. People who have witnessed a death sometimes compare it to seeing a baby being born. In one there is an incomparable moment of arrival, in the other an incomparable moment of departure. The irreversibility or sense of the finality of this moment is an important dimension of what causes distress. At the same time, many would say that the sense is profoundly one of *passing* rather than of destruction. It is not our role to

---

4 The traditional prayer for use in this situation, the *Proficiscere, anima Christiana*, is given on p. 151.

understand with completeness what is going on, not even for the clergy or the theologian. At this moment, the principal aim of the medical team will to be make this process, and its aftermath, as dignified and as peaceful as possible.

Medical frameworks

In the UK, a significant advance was the development of the Liverpool Care Pathway (LCP) in the late 1990s. This was devised by the Marie Curie Hospice in Liverpool in collaboration with the Royal Liverpool Hospital. The aim of the pathway was to bring the gold standard of end of life care practised in the hospice into the hospital setting. These guidelines were then used across the UK and internationally as an end of life care pathway. Its purpose was to provide a framework of holistic care that would integrate the work of the multi-disciplinary teams looking after dying patients and their families, including the patients' spiritual needs. It was to be used for patients thought to be in the last few days of life, once possibilities for holding off the course of their illnesses had been exhausted.

The pathway also prompted medics to consider whether some treatments should be withdrawn or withheld in the very last stages of life. There are legal frameworks surrounding such decisions. The wishes of a patient must be sought, if the patient has the capacity to express them. If not, then (in the UK and in some other countries), doctors will check to see whether there is a legally binding 'advance directive' regarding such decisions, made when the patient did have the capacity.

The LCP came under intense scrutiny following controversy in the media about its use. Much of the criticism addressed matters of feeding and hydration, sedation and other medication, and poor communication. Questions about when, and if, it is right not to feed or hydrate someone are always going to be contentious. Certainly, reduced need for food and water is part of the natural process of dying. For most patients in the terminal stage, starting artificial feeding or hydration is not appropriate and can be detrimental to the quality of dying.[5] Relatives are sometimes concerned that medication, especially medication to control pain, will accelerate death, although when used properly it does not have this effect. This topic will be covered in more detail in Chapter 9.

We have contended through this book that communication is a key. Much of the controversy surrounding the LCP centred around this: around families not knowing their relatives were dying and a lack of explanation as to what the pathway represented. Where dialogue had been good, honest and timely, this was avoided.

We have covered the story of the LCP in some detail because the issues it sought to address are important and will always be with us. As medical route map, it has been discontinued in the UK, after a review, led by Baroness Julia Neuberger, highlighted cases where it had not been used as it was intended.[6] It is to be replaced by personalized end of life 'care plans', removing the association of generic checklists and boxes to tick with the sense of a one-way 'pathway' to death. A senior physician will be involved with initiating such a care plan.

The question of how to ensure good quality care at the end of life, across a medical system, without being overly generic, is part of a developing field, and one that will be pursued slightly differently in different countries. All the same, any such guidelines and procedures are likely to reinforce the principles that we have wanted to stress in this book. In care at the end of life, it is necessary always to consider the individual, to be careful in our approach and for us all to talk more (and teach more) about the basic skills – such as the importance of compassion – that undergird care for a dying person.

---

5 Jeff Stephenson, 'The Liverpool Care Pathway', *Triple Helix*, 55 (2012), pp. 14–15.
6 Department of Health, 'More Care, Less Pathway: a review of the Liverpool Care Pathway' (15 July 2013).

Place of death

Health professionals are encouraged to talk to terminally ill patients in advance about where they would like to be cared for, come the time of their death. The aim is to give the patient choice, and others the knowledge of her wishes. All the same, situations change and the reality can be that their choice of place is not where they actually die. An initial desire to die at home might turn out not to be possible because of insufficient 'out of hours' care, because the family are exhausted or because the patient changes his or her mind. The variables are numerous. However, knowing someone's wishes is at least a good starting point and all efforts are usually made to honour this wish. Choosing the place where one is going to die is a highly meaningful process and is to be respected when possible. At the same time, one of the goals of good palliative care is to provide quality care regardless of setting.

Dying at home

Many people wish to die at home, but in fact most die in a medical institution (at least in the UK).[7] While much of the last year of life may be spent at home, most patients are admitted to hospital to die.[8] These mismatches are constantly being reviewed, but it remains the case that the elderly, the poor, those without carers and those who are geographically distant from support services are more likely to die in hospital. Dying at home requires a great deal of support, not only for the dying person but also for the family members who, most often, will be overseeing the patient's care. If this support cannot be provided, the situation will become unmanageable, and an alternative place of care must be considered, usually the local hospital or a hospice.

Where the support can be put in place, however, the familiarity of home provides a background comfort to both patients and

7 I. Higginson and G. J. Sen-Gupta, 'Place of care in advanced cancer: a qualitative systematic literature review of patient preferences', *Journal of Palliative Medicine*, 3 (2000), pp. 287–300.

8 Watson *et al.*, *Handbook of Palliative Care*, p. 842.

carers. The sights, smells, belongings and people who surround the patient are all familiar, not to mention the benefits of home cooking, while appetite remains. Pets can provide great emotional comfort and reassurance to the patient and being at home allows this dimension to continue. On the other hand, some may not want to die at home, for fear of leaving a lasting memory of the 'death bed' in the home that the family may continue to live in.

If the dying person is settled and comfortable then the chances of remaining at home are greatly increased. Most dying patients will be receiving medication to control their symptoms via a syringe driver. A district nurse will replenish this every 24 hours in accordance with a prescription from a doctor, usually the GP. A supply of medications and the required prescription may be kept in the patient's house, so that any district nurse working the relevant shift can quickly replenish the syringe driver. Regular daily contact of this kind can be a great support for patient and carers. It may not last for long, but it is likely to be a significant moment of human exchange.

Supporting a dying patient at home can be more difficult to manage if additional medication is needed between these daily visits. The carer needs to have access to telephone numbers of the district nurses, inside and outside of regular working hours. Unfortunately it can take some time for a nurse to arrive, especially during the night, when fewer nurses are on duty, or if a nurse covers a large geographical area. There are also some regions of the country where access to 24-hour district nursing care is not available, and this lack may result in a patient being admitted to a hospital or hospice, possibly some distance away from home, to enable the symptoms to be better controlled.

Some palliative care services have tried to 'plug the gap' by setting up 'hospice at home' provision. Hospice-trained nurses will, in shifts, take up residence in the patient's home, sometimes providing round the clock care. This is a remarkable but limited resource for those in the last days of life.

The basic physical needs of the patient may call for additional help with 'personal care': perhaps washing a patient, dressing and changing bedding. The principal relative may not be fit enough, physically, to carry out these essential tasks. Others may find the intimacy of washing a parent, for example, too uncomfortable. In these circumstances, professional carers come once or twice per day, which can make dying at home a possibility. This service can often be provided by social services in some countries, so it is free to the patient, but some may choose to employ carers from a private agency.

Similarly, additional equipment may be required to assist with personal care, such as a hospital-style bed, a pressure-relieving mattress, a hoist or a commode. A room may need to be re-arranged to accommodate this equipment; downstairs rooms are often converted into bedrooms, so that stairs do not have to be tackled.

Many patients will have a community palliative care nurse to co-ordinate care. The nurse is there to recognize needs and act upon them. The GP will also play an integral part in the palliative care of dying patients, in conjunction with the district nurses and the community palliative care nurse.

When it comes to dying at home, more resources and specialist support tend to be available for those who are dying from cancer than for those with other conditions, such as heart failure. Steps being taken to address this inequality include the introduction of some specialist community nurses for heart and lung conditions, and wider referral to palliative care services for non-cancer diagnoses.

Some patients and carers complain of too many 'professionals' visiting their home, but generally their presence is a great comfort, especially if it can lead to a stable and gradual process, without moments of crisis.

Relatives have spoken of the benefits of routine and rotas when caring for someone at home. Kind neighbours and members of the church congregation are often very willing to be included. Patients come to know what to expect from a routine, and at a time where so much is unknown, this can provide some stability and sense of control to the situation.

A doctor will likely find it a privilege to visit a dying person in her own home, whether as a GP or as a specialist in palliative care. The minister or other church visitor may well feel the same. It is an honour to be invited into someone's home at such time of vulnerability. You will probably be welcomed by a member of the family, a carer or a friend before being taken to the patient. It is often wise to take this opportunity to get this person's opinion, perhaps only briefly, of how he thinks the patient is doing. This can be a useful moment of contact before seeing the patient herself. A huge amount of information can also be absorbed in one visit by observing the surroundings and the dying person's interactions with carers. These are all useful indicators of physical, emotional and spiritual well-being.

Visiting someone at home involves what we are accustomed to call 'entering their personal space'. You may find the patient dressed and sitting in a favourite chair in the lounge, or you may be invited into their bedroom, where he is in bed in his nightwear. In the last days of life, he may be unconscious and no longer able to respond verbally. If you have been asked to go, then you will no doubt be made to feel welcome by the majority; most will be very grateful for your time and attentiveness. Often, just your presence will be enough to help someone feel better: the fact that you came.

It may be appropriate to see the patient alone, but take a cue from her, and from relatives. Some will prefer a family member to be present, while others will value the opportunity to talk or pray with you in private. It is often a good idea to accept a carer's offer of a cup of tea, as this can allow some private time with the patient while it is brewing. This may be the only opportunity to hear what the patient really needs to say.

The unique environment of home allows some creativity for prayers and receiving Communion. A collection of suggested prayers is included in the Appendix. Some Christians will gain comfort from the placing of a Christian image or text so that it is visible to them. Prayer cards and holding crosses can be left as comfort when you are not there.

Dying in a hospice

Despite preconceptions, terminal care is only part of the care that happens in a hospice today. Many patients are admitted for control of symptoms and then discharged home again. The care of dying patients is, however, the hallmark of the hospice movement. On a day to day basis, the staff will expect to be looking after patients in the last hours and days of their lives. They are prepared for this task.

A hospice environment is more homely than a hospital but more clinical than a home. There may be comforts such as home cooking, sofas, vases of flowers, curtains and armchairs, but also the facilities necessary for round the clock nursing and medical care.

For some, a hospice is undoubtedly the best place to die, with a team of staff looking after them, specifically trained in the field of palliative care. The ratio of nursing staff to patients is greater than on a general hospital ward, so the atmosphere is often less hurried and waiting times shorter. Beyond this, a hospice will usually have access to a broad and impressive range of professionals who will offer holistic care, not only for the dying person but also for families. This multi-disciplinary team means that there is always likely to be someone who is the best person to deal with a specific concern. If a catheter needs changing, then the nursing staff will have exactly this skill; similarly, the social work team can help a relative concerned about finances.

In most hospices, a team will hold a meeting each morning where every in-patient is discussed in turn, with the opportunity to update one another and share concerns. Specific tasks are then allocated to the member of the team deemed most appropriate to deal with them. The chaplain is often present at these daily meetings. Her non-clinical observations and insights provide an invaluable balance to the medical discussions.

When a patient is in the last days of life, members of the nursing and medical team will be allocated responsibility for the patient's care throughout a particular shift. Their role is to highlight any issues that have arisen for the patient or the family, and to ensure that the physical, emotional and spiritual needs of all are met.

This may require communication with the relevant member of the hospice team, the patient's own doctor, or, in some cases, the patient's or relatives' own priest or minister. A dying person, or relatives, should feel free to let the hospice team know if the ministry of a parish priest or chaplain would be important to them: for instance, if the patient wishes to receive the last rites. It is highly unlikely that this wish will be received with anything other than the utmost seriousness and respect.

Patients and relatives will, of course, vary in their degree of engagement with the hospice chaplain. If there is a very good relationship with the parish priest or other minister, there may be little need to speak to other clergy. Others in the same situation may be grateful for the hospice chaplain to fill the gaps between visits from the parish priest. Some patients will not welcome a visit from a chaplain at all, and have no desire to engage. Others may build a special bond with the hospice chaplain during the terminal care, along with their families, who sometimes ask the chaplain to take the funeral. Chaplains are usually very sensitive to the variations in situations, focusing on what the individual requires of them rather than adopting a blanket approach to their ministry.

For patients with a church affiliation, liaison between the parish priest or other minister and the hospice chaplain is essential. One may 'take the lead' in the relationship, which may be down to patient choice or be decided on practical grounds, such as geographical distance from home.

It can be difficult for busy clergy to attend a parishioner at the hospice to give the last rites. Knowing that a hospice chaplain is available to do so in an emergency can be of great comfort to both patients and families. The hospice will probably have access to 'on call' clergy, who will provide cover on an out of hours rota or when the chaplain is away. As we noted, it is helpful for the hospice staff to know that a patient wants the last rites, so that the time to call a priest can be best judged.

It may be only during admission to the hospice that the patient fully recognizes that she is dying. As death is acknowledged, people sometimes want to say things that have previously gone unsaid. Although this is a time of grave sickness, it can also be a period of healing and reconciliation. A hospice seeks to provide an environment that lends itself to coming to terms with the inevitable in this way. Staff are available around the clock. Indeed, it is often in the stillness of the night that patients will start to open up and talk about their hopes and fears. It can also help that the patient is, rather uniquely, surrounded by other people 'in the same boat'.

Most hospices have a combination of single rooms and bays with more than one bed. Sharing a ward means, naturally, that patients will observe other patients. Witnessing the sickness of others can provoke a number of questions. There is the natural comparison of how much better or worse one patient seems compared to another. Seeing other people in their illness can provoke an outpouring of care from one patient towards another. One patient might alert the staff using his own call bell, if he sees a fellow patient in trouble and unable to call for help. A patient may spend time sitting at the bedside of a neighbouring dying patient, or talking to relatives. Equally, relatives may gain great comfort by speaking with other relatives, and friendships form through mutual care and understanding of the other's situation.

In some hospices, a dying patient may be moved from a public ward to a single room as death approaches. This offers the family valuable privacy. Hospices will have only a few of these rooms, however, and if one is not available the patient will die on the open ward. The curtains around the bed can be closed, and comfort and reassurance can be experienced by other patients from witnessing the care that a neighbour receives in his last hours.

In the first few days after a transfer to a hospice, we may encounter a sense of failure among carers that a wish to die at home has not been fulfilled, but this is often quite quickly replaced by relief and the realization that extra support was needed. The care provided in a hospice can allow relatives to let go of the 'carer' role and just be the husband, wife, daughter, or whatever. While this can be welcome for many, others experience a need to continue in the role of care-giver in some form. If this is recognized, hospice nurses can usually find jobs with which the relative can help, so as still to be providing for their loved one.

Families vary in the degree to which they wish to be present during the last days and hours. Hospice staff are likely to stress that there is no right or wrong here. Even between members of the same family, there will be differences. Some relatives want to be present all the time and keep a bedside vigil. A camp bed or recliner chair can often be set up alongside the patient's bed to allow for this. Families may organize a rota so that the patient is never alone, but family and friends can take a break. If a patient becomes unconscious in the last dying days or hours, as is often the case, it is not uncommon for relatives to say that they feel redundant. They see no purpose in sitting beside the bed; some say that in their opinion, their loved one has 'gone already'. A theological perspective might be that the presence and value of the person does not depend on consciousness. However, it is generally right to support relatives in their own preference, as this is a deeply personal decision. Some relatives will ask not to be telephoned until the morning if the death has occurred overnight. Again, it can be important not to place any personal judgement on the decision. The important part of the care of relatives is to make sure that honest communication has happened in advance wherever possible.

Relatives who do not want to stay in the hospice are always asked if they would like to be called when death is believed to be imminent. This is promised with the caveat that the timing will not always be predictable. The hospice team will endeavour to call with sufficient time, but sometimes the patient will die before the relative arrives, or the call will turn out to be a 'false alarm'. Elderly relatives, usually a spouse, may find a call in the small hours of the night a particular shock. In this situation, and perhaps if the spouse lives alone, it may be useful to suggest that someone – in some cases from the church – can offer to stay with the spouse, or offer accompaniment travelling to the hospice.

Relatives who do not arrive in time can initially be particularly distraught, but usually find reassurance from knowing that the best care was given. Knowing that the loved one was not alone when she died, assuming that was the case, can be a particular comfort. Sitting with a dying person in the last moments, if he or she is otherwise alone, is a tremendously important act of charity that can be offered by the minister or lay visitor.

In all of this, good communication is held to be vital. Medical or nursing staff will always try to be as clear as possible about likely trajectories of events. A sense of an opportunity missed through misunderstanding or lack of information can have a long-term debilitating effect after a death.

Most hospices have a chapel or a designated quiet space where patients and relatives can spend time. In the days when a patient is dying, this place can be a haven for the friends and relatives. It can be used for personal or corporate prayer and meditation. Sometimes gentle music is played; sometimes there is silence. Resources such as prayer cards, books and poems are often available. There may be a book in which friends and relatives can write their prayer requests or simply express thoughts.

Finally, it is worth noting that every hospice has a limited number of beds, and therefore one may not be available when the patient needs it. Everything possible will be done to accommodate a patient who needs a bed for terminal care, but sometimes alternative options have to be considered.

Dying in hospital

Most deaths in the UK occur in hospital. Hospitals are therefore accustomed to caring for dying patients, whether it is sudden accidental death or a slower, more predictable death.

The introduction of hospital palliative care teams has revolutionized the care that dying patients and their relatives receive. In most hospitals, these teams do not have their own ward but act in an advisory capacity. They may, for example, be asked by a surgical ward to advise on the care of a patient who is dying from bowel cancer. Hospital palliative care teams will consist of doctors and nurses who have specialized in palliative care but have chosen to work within hospitals, rather than in a hospice or in the community. They will have access to a multi-disciplinary team within the hospital to aid in the holistic care of patients and relatives. This will usually include the hospital chaplaincy team.

The same principles of care apply as when looking after a dying person at home or in a hospice. However, dying in a hospital brings its own unique challenges. The staff on most hospital wards will have other pressing priorities, in addition to the care of the dying patient on their ward. Sticking to the surgical ward that we just mentioned as an example, nurses will also be busy preparing patients for the operating theatre and looking after post-operative patients. This is where the palliative care team can act as an advocate, highlighting the needs of the dying patient. They may suggest a plan that the medical and nursing staff on the ward can follow. This usually involves advice on medication but extends to other aspects of holistic care. It may involve the suggestion that the patient be moved into a side room, if available, to allow for a more peaceful and private environment. It could include liaison with the hospital chaplaincy team, with whom they will normally work closely. With the constant turnover of patients on a busy hospital ward, the chaplaincy team may be the ones who have the time to sit with patients and family, and listen to them with a particular degree of intention.

Clergy are always welcome to visit their parishioners or congregation in hospital. The comfort of a familiar face can be just what both patients and relatives need. Prayers can be said and tears can be shed with someone they know, in an environment where so many people are new to them. The visitor will be wise to bring along a book of prayers, especially ones for use with the sick and dying, and which include the last rites of the Church. As with visiting at home, it can be helpful to leave behind a source of hope and encouragement, whether that is a prayer card, a holding cross or an image.

Hospital visiting times are often regimented, unlike visiting at home or in a hospice, but can sometimes be relaxed to accommodate visiting those in the last days of life. Relatives might be able to stay overnight if the ward allows. This is easier if the patient is in a side room.

Some nursing and medical staff on hospital wards will have received some specific training in end of life care, so the hope is that they too will recognize the importance of the spiritual needs of their dying patient. They may initiate the contact with the hospital chaplain or clergy, rather than wait for these people to call round by chance.

Dying in a nursing home

For some people, a nursing home has been home for many years. The staff know them well and this can make a nursing home a very safe and supportive environment in which to die. Nursing homes have trained nursing staff, as opposed to residential homes, which do not.

In order for the patient to remain in the nursing home, the nursing staff will need to have received adequate training so as to be able to provide the medical and nursing care required. It is important that all the staff are educated in the care of the dying, and not only a few, to ensure 24-hour care. Nursing homes do not have district nurses attending, but staff can contact community palliative care nurses to request a visit and receive telephone advice.

Parish priests and other ministers are likely already to be regular visitors to nursing homes. These visits are opportunities to get to know the residents, so that when the person is dying, a relationship already exists.

Keeping the next of kin informed remains a priority in this setting, as in all others. Relatives may live some distance away, so timely communication is important, wherever possible. They need to be given the chance to make arrangements in order to travel to be with a dying relative in the last days, if they so wish.

Conclusion

In this chapter we have surveyed the range of settings for terminal care likely to be available in the UK and other countries. We have covered a fair amount of information in these pages, but it amounts to the outworking of some simple and fundamental principles: that the wishes of the sick person should be taken into account and followed, as far as it is possible, and that each patient should be respected as a whole person. The goals remain similar across the variety of settings, although they may not always be equally easy to achieve. Crucially, a care team will hold a variety of needs in mind, not least by recognizing the importance of relationships and promoting the well-being of family, friends and other carers. Wherever palliative care is provided, clergy and church visitors can have an important part to play in care at the end of life. In the next chapter we consider some of what the Church offers as death comes closely in view.

8

Towards the End

Forgiveness and the sacraments for the dying

In this chapter we consider preparation for death, not in general
and over the course of a life, but when death is imminent. The
practical and theological dimensions of this preparation come
together in the idea of forgiveness. Above all else, preparation
for a good death involves forgiveness. This includes forgiveness from God but also stretches to forgiveness between human
beings. Constantly, throughout the Gospels, Jesus taught that the
two – forgiveness from God and forgiveness towards one another
– are closely interwoven. The Christian message is about more
than sin, and the incarnation was more than a salvage effort, and
yet, forgiveness has always been at the centre of the Christian
proclamation. 'God was in Christ,' wrote Paul, 'not counting
people's sins against them' (2 Cor. 5.19).

The royal road to the forgiveness of sins is baptism. If someone
approaching death has not been baptized, and wants to embrace
God's offer of forgiveness in all its fullness, baptism is the answer.
Baptism need not be elaborate, and in an emergency a baptism
need consist of no more than pouring a little water over the head
with the words '[Name], I baptize you in the name of the Father,
and of the Son, and of the Holy Spirit.' Baptism can be administered by anyone. Churches with episcopal orders teach that it
is appropriate, all other things being equal, for the minister of
baptism to be a priest or deacon, or for that matter a bishop.
These people have been given a particular role to represent the
whole Church, into which the baptized person is being admitted. At a deathbed, however, all other things may not be equal.

It is good for every Christian to know that they can baptize if necessary, and how to do it.[1] When someone has already died, however, baptism is not appropriate (or, indeed, even possible).[2] The Church has held that position as universal teaching down the centuries: we cannot baptize the dead, but we can commit them into the hands of the merciful God. The majority of Christians today (as certainly all before the Reformation) are comfortable with prayers for the dead. Among recent writers, C. S. Lewis was a powerful advocate.[3] When an infant has died before baptism, although he or she cannot now be baptized, it may be appropriate for a Christian minister, or someone else, to perform some ceremony in which the child is given a name.

Most people who seek the aid of the Church at the approach of death have, however, been baptized. For them, the Church has three final sacraments: confession (or reconciliation), anointing and the Eucharist, or Lord's Supper. Confession and anointing are seen as an integral part of the approach to death for many traditions, most notably among Roman Catholics and Eastern Orthodox. Other traditions may not use these two rites quite as universally, but they are still held in honour.

Notably, drawing on our own tradition, the Book of Common Prayer urges confession of sin and absolution from a priest in the service of Visitation of the Sick, which also involves Communion of the dying. One's last Communion is known as the *viaticum*, or food for the journey. It can be profoundly helpful, and moving, for family and friends to gather to receive Communion with the dying person on this occasion.

Among many churches where anointing the sick had fallen into disuse, this rite was recognized in the twentieth century as

1 For more on emergency baptism, see Davison, *Why Sacraments?* (London: SPCK, 2013), pp. 63, 96.
2 Which is to say, were we to try to perform the rite of baptism for someone who had already died, what we did could not, in fact, be a baptism, for all it had the necessary words and actions.
3 'Of course I pray for the dead.' The action is 'spontaneous ... all but inevitable ... And I hardly know how the rest of my prayers would survive if those for the dead were forbidden ... What sort of intercourse with God could I have if what I love best were unmentionable to Him?' *Letters to Malcolm, Chiefly on Prayer* (London: Geoffrey Bles, 1964), Letter XX.

thoroughly biblical, and regained widespread use.[4] Anointing is the one sacrament oriented solely to a response to sickness. The tradition is both optimistic and circumspect about what we should expect from it: being a sacrament, the claim is that it is efficacious, and the purpose is salvation. That does not mean a short cut from suffering. Rather, through anointing we say that we want our sufferings to be understood in relation to the suffering of Christ – although what that means in practice will be different for different people. The sacrament also seeks to place the suffering person in a renewed relation to the sacraments that she received at the start of her Christian life: baptism, for all Christians, and also confirmation for many. Anointing is a sacrament of hope, but the Church is careful to stress that Christian hope ultimately lies beyond death. The body may be healed if that is conducive to salvation; but whether or not someone is healed, we can be sure of God's ultimate gift: of salvation, remission of sin, and eternal life within the family of his Son.

Towards the end: forgiving others

So far we have concentrated on forgiveness from the perspective of the relationship between a person and God. In many passages in the Gospels, Jesus connects this with the forgiveness of one person by another. We can interpret this connection in two ways, with some texts pointing in one direction and some in the other: the forgiveness of one human being by another is both the condition for forgiveness by God, and the fruit. Jesus sometimes made the rather terrifying point that God will not forgive us if we do not forgive others. This is the most likely and straightforward meaning of the words we recite, day by day, in the Lord's Prayer: 'forgive us our trespasses, *as we forgive* those who trespass against us'. Do this for us, we are saying, as we have done it for others. It behoves every Christian, therefore, to live a life both forgiving and being forgiven. As we approach death we should

---

4 For more on these sacraments, see Davison, *Why Sacraments?*, pp. 120–8, 129–41.

make particularly practical and concrete steps towards forgiving others and seeking the forgiveness of those we have wronged. (We may not receive it, but we will have asked.) The British 'Guild of All Souls', an Anglican pious society, makes the excellent suggestion that we might begin our wills with reference to these points. As they suggest it for their members:

> I die in the Holy, Catholic and Apostolic faith of our Lord Jesus Christ as it has been received and taught in the Church of England [for instance]. I commend my soul to almighty God and trusting in his mercy, implore forgiveness of all my sins. I beg forgiveness of all whom I have injured and I freely forgive those who desire forgiveness of me.

This is a good way to stress our resolve to forgive.

The warning about not forgiving, and not being forgiven, is a strong injunction to learn to forgive. However, we should recognize the depth of some wounds, and forgiveness is not always expected to come easily. Jesus spoke of forgiveness both in this life and in the world to come, and some people have suffered hurts that they may learn to forgive only later, in God's good time.

The connection between human and divine forgiveness also runs in the opposite direction. That is to say, since God has so lavishly forgiven us, we ought to forgive others. Where forgiveness is difficult, that is a good topic upon which to meditate. All this said, although the link between forgiving and being forgiven is important, salvation ultimately rests on the grace of God, and not on any work of ours. Forgiveness on our part is not a work by which we merit the grace of God.

These themes of forgiveness are so central to the teaching of Christ that they may provide a helpful line of advice for those who simply cannot embrace the Christian faith. Anyone might benefit from the suggestion that, as they leave this world, they could seek, as much as it is in their power, to be reconciled to those they have wronged, and who have wronged them. We can expect that God delights when anyone reaches out in search of forgiveness, however hazy their sense of God might be.

Towards the end: almsgiving

We have already mentioned the Prayer Book service for the Visitation of the Sick. It contains several practical suggestions. For instance, the dying person is encouraged to put his house in good order. This is one way in which we honour our family and friends – taking the commandments to honour father and mother (Exod. 20.12; Eph. 6.2), and interpreting this in terms of wider family obligations – by making sure that our affairs can be taken up relatively easily by those who will administer them. When we make a will, we might also remember the injunction, also in the Prayer Book, to remember the poor, and not only our friends and kin. Only the most hardened capitalist would disagree that the making of money can be a somewhat grubby and compromising endeavour, and that it often is. Historically speaking, most readers of this book will live in countries where current wealth and prosperity rest to some extent upon exploitative practices in days gone by, of which slavery is the most obvious example. The prosperity we enjoy and the money we may leave at death have not been accumulated without leaving some scars. It is therefore appropriate – all thought of salvation by works properly put aside – to contribute to the relief of those who have come off less well from the financial balance of power. In addition, just as we have supported the work of the Church in life, we can support it in death.

Almsgiving in our will is a properly Christian discipline, and the practice of drawing up the necessary document can be usefully sobering. It is certainly a preparation for death. All the same, a will can remain to us no more than ink on a page. The Church teaches not only a proper disposal of our goods after death but also a proper sense of detachment from worldly goods during life. St Catherine of Genoa wrote eloquently about this, and described detachment as a process we have to go through, either in this life or thereafter.[5] The point is not to *despise* the good things of this world, as that would be to value God's good gifts too lightly. The aim, rather, is to treat them for what they are: gifts that

---

5 'Purgation and Purgatory' in *Purgation and Purgatory: The Spiritual Canticle* (New York: Paulist Press, 1979).

point beyond themselves to the divine giver; passing gifts, given to recipients able to enjoy them only temporarily. We can foster a proper sense of detachment, by which we more or less mean 'perspective', by giving a sacrificially significant portion of our income away, by exploring ways to 'fast' from involvement in a consumerist culture during Lent, and by every activity and relationship that fixes our attention outside of ourselves and reminds us that our good and happiness is bound up with the good and happiness of others.

At the end: facing death[6]

We naturally fear death. To fear death as a Christian, however, can feel like fraud or failure. There is, however, no shame in it. We should not want to encourage anyone to be unnecessarily distressed (while admitting that if death has a sobering influence on some people, that can be a good thing), but we might want to reassure the dying person that an apprehension that cannot be banished is not a sign of failure or divine displeasure.

As confirmation of this, we can turn to Christ himself. Before his death, in Gethsemane, Christ became 'grieved and agitated' at the prospect of what was to come (Matt. 26.37; Mark 14.33 has 'distressed and agitated'). As he prayed in 'anguish', his sweat 'became like great drops of blood falling down on the ground' (Luke 22.44). This may refer to the profusion of normal sweat, or even that in his distress his sweat became mingled with blood (as can very rarely occur through stress-related breaking of fine blood vessels).[7] As his death drew near, Christ – the incarnate Son of God – was afraid.

Among the later Church Fathers, Maximus the Confessor holds pre-eminent status here, for having explored the meaning of the incarnation to new depths. He stressed that Christ had a human fear of death, since Christ was fully human. Christ transformed

---

6 See above, pp. 19–20, for a discussion of Christ's last words from the cross in relation to death.

7 The Greek, *hosei*, favours the second interpretation.

this fear, in the sense that he deployed all that he was for our sake, and offered everything to the Father, but that does not take away the fact that he experienced fear.[8] Alternatively, we might come at this from another angle, with another seventh-century theologian, Anastasius of Sinai. He put it differently: not that Christ feared death but that he hated it, and its prospect.[9] If we hate the prospect of death, we are in good company. Nor should the onlooker fear to grieve. As the shortest verse in the Bible (at least in the Authorized Version) reminds us, 'Jesus wept' (John 11.35).

We might also add that the Christian need not worry about whether she is particularly able to conceptualize or visualize the life of the world to come. Many images of that future life have been given us, and different images comfort different people. All said, they are just that: images. For that reason, for some they may seem as much to veil as to reveal. In that case, we need only go to the heart of them, which is to say that whatever the life of the world to come looks like, it is about being close to God. In the words of Janet Soskice, 'Many regard "what happens next" as a quiet horizon of hope – another aspect of the trust in God they experience in daily life but not necessarily highly theorized.'[10] That is fine.

We cannot magic fear away. Rather, the central message as we approach death is one echoed throughout the New Testament: God is with us, whatever we are going through (see Matt. 1.23; 14.23; 18.20; 28.20; John 1.14; Rom. 5.5). Favourite words from Romans 8 are particularly relevant: 'For I am convinced that neither death, nor life, nor angels, nor rulers, nor things present, nor things to come, nor powers, nor height, nor depth, nor any-

---

8 For instance, *Opuscule* 7 (8-C-D), as quoted by Blowers and Wilken in *Cosmic Mystery of Jesus Christ*, p. 176, footnote 4. In the *Disputation with Pyrrhus*, Maximus wrote that if Christ's fear was different from ours (in that we cannot choose but fear, whereas Christ took on all that is ours voluntarily), then this means not that he feared less, but that his fear surpassed ours.

9 *Sermones duo in constitutionem hominis secundum imaginem Dei*, which has not been translated into English.

10 'Dying Well in Christianity', in Harold G. Coward and Kelli I. Stajduhar (eds), *Religious Understandings of a Good Death in Hospice Palliative Care* (Albany: State University of New York Press, 2012), pp. 123–44, p. 133.

thing else in all creation, will be able to separate us from the love of God in Christ Jesus our Lord' (Rom. 8.38–39).

God is with us as our creator and the source of our being, from moment to moment. God is present by the Holy Spirit, and through Christ, not least as head of his body, the Church. God is with us in the sacraments, and through the scriptures. God is present in the love and care of family, friends and those who look after us. Christ is present as the one who 'died and was buried' and who has therefore been with us in death. Indeed, Christ knows death in both of the two senses we outlined in Chapter 2: dying and being dead. He knows death in the first sense, since Jesus knew an agonizing death, and he stands beside us as one who knew spiritual anguish ('My God, my God, why have you forsaken me?' – Matt. 27.46) as well as the physical pain of crucifixion. Jesus also stands alongside us as one who has been dead. As we noted in Chapter 2, just as the words from the Creed '[he] died' are an astonishing witness to God's solidarity with humanity, so too are the words '[he] was buried'. As Jesus had said, 'for three days and three nights the Son of Man will be in the heart of the earth' (Matt. 12.40).[11]

These are mysteries hard to fathom. Before moving on, here are two meditations on God's being-with-us in Christ, even in death. The first is from St Irenaeus of Lyons, the second from the nineteenth-century hymn-writer William Dalrymple Maclagan.

He [Christ] did not reject humanity or go beyond its limitations, nor did he set aside for Himself that law which He had appointed for the human race. Rather, He sanctified each stage of life, by making possible a likeness to himself. For He came to save all through his own person – all, I say, who through Him are born again to God – infants, and children, and boys and girls, and youths, and old men and women. He therefore passed through every age ... Then, at last, He came even to death itself, that He might be 'the first-born from the dead, that in all things

---

11 The counting is not askew. 'Three days and three nights' refers to Jonah, and as a span of time, Jewish reckoning would have counted three parts of days (with their 'nights' associated here for effect) as whole days.

He might have the pre-eminence,' the Author of Life, who goes before all and shows the way.[12]

It is finished! Blessed Jesus,
thou hast breathed thy latest sigh,
teaching us, the sons of Adam,
how the Son of God must die.

Lifeless lies the piercèd body,
hidden in its rocky bed,
laid aside like folded garment:
where is now the Spirit fled?

In the gloomy realms of darkness
shines a light unknown before,
for the Lord of dead and living
enters at the open door.

See! he comes a willing victim,
unresisting hither led;
passing from the cross of sorrow
to the mansions of the dead.

Lo! the heavenly light around him
as he draws his people near;
all amazed they stand rejoicing
at the gracious words they hear.

For himself proclaims the story
of his own incarnate life,
and the death he died to save us,
victor in that awful strife.

---

12 St Irenaeus of Lyons, *Against Heresies*, II.xxii.4. Translation from Henry Bettenson, *Early Christian Fathers* (Oxford: Oxford University Press, 1956), with emendations.

Patriarch and priest and prophet
gather round him as he stands,
in adoring faith and gladness,
hearing of the piercèd hands.

O the bliss to which he calls them,
ransomed by his precious Blood,
from the gloomy realms of darkness
to the Paradise of God!

There in lowliest joy and wonder
stands the robber at his side,
reaping now the blessèd promise
spoken by the Crucified.

Jesus, Lord of dead and living,
let thy mercy rest on me;
grant me too, when life is finished,
rest in Paradise with thee.

William Dalrymple Maclagan, 1875

Preparation for death is a strange sort of thing. Almost every other sort of preparation we work at is preparation for something that we are going to *do*. Death, however, is something that happens to us. Preparation usually involves action and control but here we are preparing for the end of action, or agency: for relinquishment of control.[13] We might say that at our last moment everything – the whole universe – is contracted to Paul's three 'theological virtues': faith, hope and love (1 Cor. 13.13).

---

13 The twentieth-century Dominican Edward Schillebeeckx wrote perceptively about this in his essay 'The Death of a Christian' (p. 76). The way to respond, he suggested, to this event that is not our own action, is threefold: first in 'obedient love', saying 'let this be' according to your will; second, in 'contrition', saying 'this is just and fitting', since we are sinners and, however well we have lived, we are in solidarity with the whole human race, in its wrongdoing; third, in a 'being emptied out of self in union with Christ', saying 'my God and my all': a motto of the Franciscans.

We can start with faith. Faith is a human act – we 'have faith' – but, fortunately, it is more than our action. Ultimately, it is *trust* and it does not rest on our own strength, or force of will, but on God. Christian faith, in the last analysis, is *faith in* the faithfulness *of God*; Christian trust, in the last analysis, is trust in his trustworthiness. Meeting death in faith is therefore not about flexing some 'faith muscle' very hard; it is the assurance that when our last ability to act or think ebbs away, we can rest in God.

This is even more obvious with hope, since hope is clearly always *in* something. Christianity does not celebrate hope without an object; rather, it celebrates hope in God. Hope, we read in Hebrews, is an anchor for the soul (Heb. 6.19). The point about an anchor is not what is going on at our end of the rope, but at the end that the anchor holds securely. Hope, as an anchor, secures us because of what it is lodged in. Hope is about being lodged in God, in life and in death.

When we come to love, the greatest of this trio, we are with God from the beginning. Indeed, the love of God is all about God taking the initiative. The crucial thing is not our love of God but God's love for us: 'In this is love, not that we loved God but that he loved us and sent his Son' (1 John 4.10). This love was what led God to create the world in the first place; it is the love that sought us out, and that love will bring us home. It may be a comfort, in death, to realize that we return to the one whose love preceded, and caused, our very existence.

Preparation for death is indeed odd, being preparation for something that is no act of ours. We practise for it, all the same, by living a life of surrender to God. Even for the holiest of us, perhaps, letting go will be difficult. It is made easier if there is someone with us to hold our hand. On that basis, it should be the earnest desire of the Church to be present – through her sons and daughters – with the dying, wherever and whenever that ministry can be extended. That way, we bear witness to the words of St Anthony of Egypt: 'My life and my death are with my neighbour.'

9

'I Just Want to Die'

As we write this chapter, euthanasia and 'assisted dying' remain emotive and hotly debated topics. News reports (certainly in the UK) tend to stress the position of those in favour of a change in the law to legalize these acts. That would put the UK alongside countries such as the Netherlands. Representatives of the churches, and of other religions, typically oppose such changes.

It will be helpful to begin with some definitions. Euthanasia can be defined as 'the intentional killing by act or omission of a person whose life is felt not to be worth living'.[1] It is intentional killing, by act or omission, of a dependent human being, for that person's alleged benefit. The word 'intentional' here is crucial. If death is not intended, it is not an act of euthanasia. We call euthanasia 'voluntary' when the person who is killed has requested to be killed.

We can distinguish between euthanasia and suicide. Suicide is the act of taking one's own life voluntarily and intentionally. With euthanasia, the person who is killing is not the person who is killed; with suicide, the person performing the 'act' that leads to death is the same person who dies. Suicide is 'assisted' if someone else provides the person committing suicide with the information, guidance, or means to take his own life, and if they do so with the intention that what they provide will be used for that purpose. As an example, a pharmacist would not be party to assisted suicide if she provided a drug, not knowing the purpose

---

1 Tim Maughan, 'Euthanasia', *Christian Medical Fellowship File*, 22 (2003).

for which it was going to be used, but she would be party if she knew. When a doctor helps someone to kill himself, this is called 'physician-assisted suicide'. As we write this book, euthanasia is legal in Belgium, Luxembourg and the Netherlands, and assisted suicide is legal in the latter two countries, Switzerland and some US states.

Euthanasia is most frequently carried out by a doctor administering lethal drugs, usually by injection. This differs from physician-assisted suicide, where the doctor provides the means of killing by prescribing lethal medication, but the patient administers it himself. The *assistance* is in providing the means.

We sometimes read about 'passive euthanasia', a term used to describe a death resulting from an action (or a decision not to act) where the primary intention was not to cause death. The term is unhelpful, even nonsensical. For an act to be euthanasia, there has to be intention to cause death. A sensible medical decision, taken for the sake of safeguarding quality of life, cannot be euthanasia. A doctor, patient or relative is nowhere near euthanasia if she chooses not to start a treatment that would, in any case, provide no benefit to the patient. Nor are we talking about euthanasia if a treatment is withdrawn that has been shown to be ineffective or burdensome, or is unwanted. These are all part of good medical practice. To call them euthanasia muddies the waters and steals respectability for euthanasia from ethical clinical life.

In discussing this emotive and complex subject, it is perhaps best for us to concentrate on bringing our own experience (here Sioned's) of working at the front line with people who are dying, and to bring that into dialogue with the theological traditions of the Church.

Among those who are dying, we come across a wide spectrum of reactions to impending death. Sometimes, although very rarely, there is euphoria. Paul wrote: 'For to me, living is Christ and dying is gain ... my desire is to depart and be with Christ, for that is far better' (Phil. 1.21, 23). Others exhibit a serene acceptance, and a sense of patient waiting. Euphoria aside, this is perhaps what we would want for everyone: being at peace, reconciled with God and one's neighbours, waiting trustfully. Sometimes acceptance is more *resigned* than *serene*. These patients have a 'matter of fact' approach to what is happening. Death is clearly not what they want, but that is what is happening, and there is no point fighting the inevitable.

Others wait impatiently. This response is often accompanied by the frequent asking of questions such as 'How long have I got?', usually out of fear not of having too little time but that dying will take too long. They can see no purpose in living longer but are usually easily comforted or distracted. Waiting can also make people angry. In particular, someone may move from waiting impatiently to anger and resentfulness that they have not yet died. If single-minded enough, they may make an active decision to refuse food and water in an attempt to accelerate the process.

In a few cases, people are regretful that they have become too weak to travel to somewhere where assisted suicide is legal. Patients may ask for the doctors to help them die, but this happens infrequently.

In every case, across the spectrum of these responses, we encounter a human being facing death. Those who are at peace may be at the end of a journey of exploration, supported along the way by loved ones and professionals. For the remainder, time is needed to listen to and 'witness' their suffering. We need to explore this suffering in all its various dimensions – physical, emotional and spiritual – and do all we can to ease it.

We would both oppose any change in the law to legalize assisted suicide, although we are aware of other Christians who are in favour of a change to the law, who hold a contrasting interpretation of what it means for the Christian to be called to love and compassion. We understand why people ask for such change, but we do not believe that assisted suicide is the proper expression of compassion. Our experience is that, given the time and attention the patient needs and deserves, most people begin to let go of their requests for an accelerated death. Sioned remembers a patient recounting that she only received the help that she needed after, out of desperation, requesting assisted suicide. Obviously, it is terrible that she had to go to such extreme lengths in order to be listened to properly.

When dying people have received attentive care and compassion, they have often been able to find new meaning to their lives and have regained some hope for the time they have left, however long that may be. We have witnessed dying people say, rather chillingly, that they now count their blessings that holistic, compassionate palliative care was there when they needed it, as had assisted suicide been a legal option, they would have taken it and subsequently missed some precious time with their families.

All this said, there remain those who, regardless of good palliative care, continue to request an assisted death. This is a real challenge. At present, we can legitimately say that it is against the law for any doctor to accelerate someone's death in any way. Medical teams continue to offer all they can to relieve suffering, but we should acknowledge that in a small number of cases this does not alleviate the patient's desire to die. Some patients doubt the integrity of the term 'holistic care' when such requests are rejected. The doctor is placed here in a profoundly difficult position since she will always wish to listen to a patient and, wherever possible, to address the needs and desires of each individual who is dying. However, when that desire is illegal, and it conflicts with the ethos of those caring for the patient, the situation can become very difficult. While a doctor will respond in every way possible, that cannot be on the terms this patient might wish.

Baroness Ilora Finlay of Llandaff, a professor of palliative medicine, recounts the story of her own mother's request to be helped to die.[2] The hospice chaplain played a transformational role, which gave her mother reason to carry on living and to do so with renewed meaning.

It was the hospice chaplain who unlocked the door. Wise enough to realise there was no point talking about God to this agnostic lady and experienced enough to know we all have a story, he quietly and patiently asked Mum to tell him hers.

And so he sat, this quiet, unassuming man, and listened, soaking up the years, as she told him her views and philosophy on life.

2 *Daily Mail*, 19 March 2010.

And it was in this telling that it dawned on Mum that her decrepit body still held an active mind. Suddenly, she realised that if she wasn't going to be allowed to kill herself, she had better make the most of what time remained.
She went on to live for another four years.

Those who campaign for legalized euthanasia and assisted dying take human rights, choice and control as the central themes of their argument.[3] They hold that competent adults with a terminal illness should have the right to decide the time and manner of their death. They too give anecdotal evidence, of witnessing prolonged suffering first-hand, as the prime motivation for their campaign: heart-wrenching accounts of loss of control and dignity, perhaps during a protracted neurological degenerative disease such as motor neurone disease, or more generally at the terminal care stage of other diseases. They hope for a change in the law to allow competent terminally ill adults to die quickly when they decide that life is not worth living.

Those who oppose euthanasia and assisted suicide put the emphasis on possibilities, potential and importance of good palliative care and the likely disastrous consequences that would come from changing the law.[4] Rowan Williams, then Archbishop of Canterbury, expressed his concerns about a change in the law to the Church of England's General Synod in February 2012:

We are committed, as Christians, to the belief that every life in every imaginable situation is infinitely precious in the sight of God. To say that there are certain conditions in which life is legally declared to be not worth living is a major shift in the moral and spiritual atmosphere in which we live. We can

---

3 Represented in the UK, for instance, by campaigning group, Dignity in Dying.

4 In the UK, Care Not Killing is a UK-based alliance of individuals and organizations which brings together disability and human rights groups, healthcare providers, and faith-based bodies, with the aims of promoting more and better palliative care, ensuring that existing laws against euthanasia and assisted suicide are not weakened or repealed and influencing the balance of public opinion against any further weakening of the law.

be realistic, we can be compassionate in the application of the existing law ... [However, to legalize assisted suicide and euthanasia would be,] I believe, to change something vital in our sense of the value of life itself.[5]

He echoed this when he wrote that 'legal recognition of a liberty to decide the moment of one's death, and to require professional assistance in securing this, shifts what we might call the "default setting" of a society'.[6]

Christians believe in a duty to protect the vulnerable. In large measure, this is one purpose of the legal system. An individual request for physician-assisted suicide and euthanasia should be seen in the light of a bigger picture, and the impact of legalization on the moral compass of society. If the protective boundary that currently exists is rubbed out, we can expect consequences to follow similar to those that have followed in countries where physician-assisted suicide and euthanasia are legal. Those who feel a burden to their families, and society more widely, begin to feel pressure to opt for assisted dying, not for their own sake but for the sake of others (as they see it). Those born with disabilities have raised concerns that their lives will be viewed as 'not worth living' in some circumstances. Three years after codifying the law, allowing euthanasia for adult patients in the Netherlands, Dutch doctors adopted guidelines for the 'mercy killing' of newborn babies.[7] Evidence suggests that financial beneficiaries with ill-intent can manipulate the time of a parent's death (for instance) to their own advantage.[8]

The harsh reality of what is involved in the act of physician-assisted suicide is not widely known. According to medical evidence, the 'controlled and dignified death' advertised by clinics

---

5 Address to Church of England's General Synod, February 2012.
6 Rowan Williams, 'Reconnecting Human Rights and Religious Faith', in *Faith in the Public Square* (London: Bloomsbury, 2012), p. 166.
7 'Dutch doctors adopt guidelines on mercy killing of newborns', *British Medical Journal*, 331 (2005), p. 126.
8 'Beating the deadline', *The Economist*, 25 November 2010; Joshua S. Gans and Andrew Leigh, 'Did the Death of Australian Inheritance Taxes Affect Deaths?', *Topics in Economic Analysis & Policy*, 6 (2006), article 23.

and campaigners is by no means guaranteed. The medication pre-scribed for assisted suicide is a massive overdose of barbiturates. These are not the drugs used in palliative care to ease suffering. The failure rate has been reported as 16 per cent,[9] which is high for any medical intervention. When death does not occur, the con-sequences are distressing for all concerned. In the Netherlands, a failed attempt would require the doctor to carry out euthanasia with a lethal injection, in order to ensure that death occurs. In other countries, where euthanasia is not legal, the patient may take several days to die, or be left in a persistent vegetative state. In one case, a woman was transferred from the Dignitas clinic in Zurich back to the UK in such a condition. On this basis, as physician-assisted suicide is sometimes 'unsuccessful', there would be an inbuilt tendency towards legalizing euthanasia, fol-lowing the legalization of physician-assisted suicide, in order to give a doctor the authority to kill a patient whose own attempt has failed.

In the Netherlands, the Royal Dutch Association of Pharmacy provides prescribing guidelines that aim to increase the efficiency of assisted suicide. Nonetheless, there are still problems, as was demonstrated in a study of 649 cases in the Netherlands.[10] These were reported as technical errors, complications and situations where the patient either took a long time to die, or indeed did not die at all. Technical errors included difficulties in finding a vein to inject the drugs into, or in swallowing the prescribed medication. Complications were listed as nausea, vomiting, muscle spasms, and in some cases extreme gasping. The most common problems with 'completion' were a longer than expected interval between the administration of medication and death, and failure to induce a comatose state. It is known that in the Netherlands not all assisted suicides are reported, so the percentage of complications may well be far greater.

---

9 Johanna H. Groenewoud *et al.*, 'Clinical Problems with the Performance of Euthanasia and Physician-Assisted Suicide in the Netherlands', *New England Journal of Medicine*, 342 (2000), pp. 551–6.

10 Groenewoud *et al.*, 'Clinical Problems'.

Rowan Williams has spoken of the vulnerability of doctors who are asked to assist in a patient's death.[11] We should all be concerned about the damage to the doctor–patient relationship that would occur if physician-assisted suicide were to be legalized. The dynamic would be profoundly changed. Doctors are trained to heal, not to harm: to cure not to kill. Sioned has been humbled by the trust people have placed in her to do good. The majority, but not all, of doctors in front-line palliative care are against physician-assisted suicide. For some doctors, this 'treatment option' would make their role unsustainable. As the Hippocratic Oath puts it, they live by the principle that 'I will neither give a deadly drug to anybody if asked for it, nor will I make a suggestion to this effect.'

In her role as a palliative care doctor, Sioned has witnessed suffering of all kinds eased by specialist, holistic intervention, and seen patients find renewed purpose, for however short a time they have left. We see people able to accept that *less* – whether that be in terms of time, independence or ability – is not the same as the *loss* of their worth or their value as a human being. As Rowan Williams has put it:

> If we ask what is protected by a change in the law, it is not easy to answer ... [Moreover, the religious believer is likely to hold that] life is not to be surrendered in this way because every imaginable condition is capable of being lived through in a way that relates it to God ... [F]aced with the possibility of a change to the law that is designed to protect a supposed liberty at the cost of removing a highly significant protection for the most vulnerable, I do not believe we can claim that this is straightforwardly about honouring a universal entitlement.[12]

11 Address to General Synod.
12 Address to General Synod.

A personal story from Sioned

During my first year after qualifying as a doctor, and many years before specializing in palliative care, I witnessed unbearable suffering in an elderly woman who was dying, as her daughter watched helplessly. At that early stage in my career, I had relatively little experience of knowing how to manage her terminal distress. I am sure that if this were the only experience I could recall, I would be signing up to the campaign for assisted dying. However, I now know a different approach is possible. The way forward is for more provision, more education and wider availability of good palliative care in all settings.

People are still experiencing avoidable distressing deaths in this country, as in other countries around the world. Part of the solution is awareness of what is possible and can be provided. That would reduce the number of incidents like the one I witnessed, which are disproportionately reported in the media. That is one of my motives, and Andrew's, for writing this book.

I am not naive and I do not think that all suffering will be fully relieved. The focus, nonetheless, should be on ending suffering rather than ending lives. Clergy and other church visitors have a significant role to play in this.

10

Caring for the Carers

Communication with carers

Talking to the relatives, friends and carers of a patient is an important part of the work of a palliative care doctor: perhaps more important than is often recognized. The Christian minister or other visitor can also usefully show concern for those who attend the dying person.

Not all carers are family members. Some may be neighbours; some are friends; others are formal, paid carers. Fortunately, very few people have no carers: most developed societies have a system for flagging up those most vulnerable and in need of care. That said, there will be a variation in the 'quantity' of care that someone receives and in the extent to which it draws upon pre-existing relationships. Some people care out of love, some out of duty and others because it is their profession. Regardless of the person or motive, caring for those who care is essential.

In caring for the carers, we are also helping those who are sick, who may feel guilty on account of the 'burden' they think they represent. They may see people around them struggling with a physical task, or having to take on roles to which they are not accustomed. Sickness can bring about a reversal: the once-carer becomes the cared-for. We should not underestimate the extent to which this adjustment can throw up significant challenges. Tasks that have been the rite (or right) of one party have to be relinquished: driving or overseeing finances (even simply writing cheques), for example. Often this occurs within a couple but, in a similar vein, children may become carers for one of their parents and forgo the dependent role that was previously part of their identity.

Normally, one person is highlighted as the main carer. This person will be the one who has the most information to offer concerning the well-being of the patient, and the one most closely involved in day to day care. Working out who best fulfils this role is an important task, and should take into account a sense of who else is involved in care, and how the carers relate. Usually, this is clear and straightforward to establish. Occasionally, however, we encounter a battle for this authoritative and representative position. In such a situation, the medical team will wish to obtain additional perspectives, not least from the patient and other professionals involved.

The main carer is usually also the next of kin, especially if the patient is elderly, but this is not always the case. In a large family or circle of friends, it can be useful to ask them to nominate a 'spokesperson', who can relay information on to others. This may, indeed, already have happened naturally. Such an arrangement avoids falling into the situation, potentially confusing and conflicting, where information is repeated to numerous relatives and friends. As well as providing clarity for the medical team, this sort of delineation can help where family politics would risk conflicting responses.

All involved with the care of the dying – both medical and other pastoral figures – should avoid any sense of collusion with patients and carers against each other. Many patients and carers will, out of a sense of protectiveness, ask that news regarding the illness is not shared with another party. This can lead to tangles, indeed to farce. Honesty is always the best policy. As we noted in Chapter 6, the best approach can be not to share news unprompted but to be clear with all parties that every question asked will be answered honestly, although, of course, as sensitively as possible. We may find both the patient and the carer asking for the other to be protected from news of which they are both in fact aware. Encouraging honest communication in this situation can be refreshing. The better such communication proceeds, the easier it is for people to offer one another mutual support when it is most needed. The medical team is likely to want to follow the good principle, when it comes to breaking bad news, of offering the opportunity for someone else to be with a patient when new information is shared. That might involve inviting the next of kin or carer to be present, although sometimes a member of the clergy or church visitor might be called upon to fulfil this role. Working this way serves several purposes. It makes sure that the relevant parties hear the news at the same time, avoiding any sense of collusion; it means that a second pair of ears can take the information in and, importantly, it fosters mutual support.

Communication with carers is paramount but it is always preferable, wherever possible, to obtain the patient's consent beforehand about sharing information about her illness with the family and carers.

The needs of carers

Studies of informal carers have identified that one of their greatest needs is to be well informed.[1] With knowledge comes a greater sense of control. They need to know about the diagnosis and what to expect as the illness progresses. It is also reassuring to know which services can be contacted, especially 'out of hours'.

Although anxiety and depression are common among carers looking after someone in the last months of life, there are many practical ways to assist them. These have been summarized as 'practical and domestic, psychosocial, financial and spiritual'.[2]

Carers at home

Without the support of carers, many patients would be unable to stay at home, and yet caring for someone who is dying at home can be exhausting, both emotionally and physically. Attending to

---

1 Amanda Ramirez, Julia Addington-Hall and Michael Richards, 'ABC of Palliative Care: The Carers', *British Medical Journal*, 316 (1998), p. 208.

2 Ramirez *et al.*, 'ABC of Palliative Care', p. 208.

the well-being of the carer, who is usually a spouse, partner or adult child, is therefore particularly significant, not least for the patient.

Carers who are fit enough may be willing and able to take on these roles, but professional carers are available to help. They may only be able to visit sporadically, however, usually in the form of two, possibly three, short visits a day. This will leave the principal carer alone for many hours, and the visits from a professional will not always coincide with the times of greatest need. Night-sitters are a scarce but valuable resource, available for some patients but usually only for a limited number of nights.

The patient will usually be bed-bound and frail. He may be strong enough to move with assistance to a chair, but a hoist may be required for this to be possible. The patient, in short, becomes increasingly dependent over time for all of her physical needs.

The church visitor cannot resolve all of the problems that may present themselves, by any means. We can, however, do a great deal of good by asking the carer *how he or she is* and by representing a connection to a wider community. Our questions, expressions of concern and discussion of options can bring perspective. Carers might, for instance, recognize for the first time quite how tired they have become, and decide to ask for additional help. This might lead to a review of the medication and equipment needed for the patient's treatment at home.

Above all, what we may be able to offer best is a willingness to sit and listen. Carers may not have many people to whom they can 'off-load'. If they are members of your congregation, whom you know well, your existing relationship can offer enormous insights into the back-story of what is going on, and make for particularly supportive conversations.

A carer's life is likely to change frequently and an imminent loss lies ahead. This can be the cause of much anxiety, although this is frequently suppressed. Carers may deny their own needs in preference to the needs of the one cared for, and will often be reluctant to talk about stresses or 'complaints' since the patient is seen as one who needs attention. We will hear carers say that they will have time 'afterwards' to deal with their needs. This approach risks physical and emotional exhaustion, after which they will find it increasingly difficult to manage. Carers need to hear that they matter *now*. The visitor may also be able to offer some perspective on how to find some respite from the burdens of care. As an example, a home often feels 'taken over' by equipment and medication. Perhaps what had once been a family dining room is now a clinical zone. Making a place of retreat within the house, which feels like 'home', can be restorative. As mentioned, carers may also be more able to cope if they simply know who to contact in an emergency. Having a list of numbers on the fridge or by the phone can build a sense of confidence when the carer is alone.

Sometimes carers are able to organize a rota of family and friends to help, so that the principal carer can have a break. It can be very helpful if a church is able to contribute to such a rota. Other practical help, such as dog walking, grocery shopping, providing meals or help with laundry, could also feature on such a rota within a family, church fellowship or community. We should note that some patients feel insecure if their main carer is out of the house, even if another person is with them. Introducing other people as familiar helpers as early in the illness as possible can help to avoid this anxiety.

Ultimately, there may come a time when the needs of the patient become incompatible with staying at home. An alternative place of care is needed, usually a hospice or hospital.

Carers in a hospice

'Guilty', 'relieved', 'sidelined' or 'grateful': these are all words we hear from carers when a loved one is transferred to a hospice. For many, the response is principally one of grateful relief from the pressure and struggles experienced at home. Hospice care provides round-the-clock specialist attention from a multi-disciplinary team. Carers usually feel that their loved one is in good hands and that they can sleep in peace at night, feeling that the burden of care is being shouldered by an expert and caring team. There may

CARING FOR THE CARERS

be a sense of failure, however, that they were unable to keep the dying person at home. In this situation it can be useful to express recognition of the care that carers have given to date in some explicit way. Ideally, the carer will find 'permission' now to revert to being the wife, for example, rather than the carer. The hospice staff can take that responsibility from her.

We need to be sensitive to the carers who feel sidelined and redundant, for whom the transition is principally that of having something 'taken from them'. They may look on with disagreement as to the way in which care is now being given, especially if a very different routine has been introduced. Even here, and perhaps all the more so, it is important that the carer has a voice. The medical and nursing teams will want to take time to hear how things were done at home: what worked well and what the reasons were for admission, which now need addressing. Hospice staff will often try to address this feeling of loss of control by offering the carer a chance to join in the personal care of the patient, or at least in asking them if they have any suggestions as to how that care could be provided.

Carers are likely to appreciate time to talk through the roller coaster of emotions they are experiencing after an admission, and a church visitor can help here. An opportunity to speak to the hospice chaplain may be welcome, although those who are not used to clergy in their daily lives may feel threatened and uncomfortable by such an offer. Most hospice chaplains have perfected an unobtrusive and non-coercive style. They are present and visible on the ward and will just 'pass by' with a welcome smile or gentle greeting, which offers a response, but does not force it. If a carer is of a different faith or denomination from the chaplain, one that is not represented among the hospice in-patient team, a chaplain can contact a local leader to assist within the hospice.

Hospital and hospice chaplains usually value a close working relationship with local clergy and church volunteers. If a member of your congregation is a carer, or a patient in hospital or a hospice, speak to the chaplain. Keeping the care of the patient and carers as the central motive will avoid any unnecessary politics or tensions, rare though these are. Before information is shared, it is worth obtaining the permission of patient or carer. This also applies to announcements in church.

Hospices have rooms allocated for private discussions, where the chaplain or visiting minister can meet a relative or carer alone if needed. There will be a chapel or quiet space too, where relatives and friends can spend time alone or with others reflecting, praying, crying or expressing emotions away from the patient. Some hospices hold services, which carers can be encouraged to attend if they so wish. Hospice facilities for patients, which might include complementary therapies such as massage, are often available to carers as well. We can alert carers in need to this fact.

A hospice may be some distance from the parish or congregation from which the carer comes. In that case, the hospice chaplain may take the lead in the care of the carer during admission. The distance from the hospice may provide another opportunity for friends, family and parishioners to help: perhaps in the task of driving carers to and fro, or in contributing to a rota for sitting with the patient.

If the patient stabilizes during the admission, the question arises as to where the most appropriate place of care has now become. Again, it is essential that the main carer plays a part in this decision process. Returning home, perhaps with additional help, is one option, as is admission to a nursing home. These are not easy decisions and many people will appreciate the opportunity to talk over the 'pros' and 'cons', and the mixed feelings, that accompany such a decision. Despite even well-made plans, patients sometimes deteriorate before the planned date of discharge and die in the hospice after all. Again, good communication from the hospice team, and a listening ear from those with pastoral responsibilities, is essential.

If admission to the hospice is for terminal care, attention will centre around the remaining precious few days. Carers must be free to choose how they spend these last days and hours. Some will wish not to leave the bedside, as we have already mentioned, while others will feel no need to do this and will continue to come to visit for a short time each day. There should be no sense of judgement as to an individual's decisions.

Carers in hospital

Being in hospital, whether as a patient or a visitor, can be a disempowering experience. The round of activity can be relentless and monotonous; it can be difficult to identify who is who on the ward, and which person on a particular shift is responsible for the care of a particular patient: everyone, and no one, can seem to have that role. Many staff members will wish that they had more time to get to know individual patients and families but the workload and paperwork can prevent that.

Carers at a distance

When family members do not live close to the dying person, for instance if a patient is in a nursing home at a considerable distance from even the closest family, or when relatives live abroad, the role of clergy and lay visitors with the family will be modest. Principally, we can encourage people to keep lines of communication open. Family members may find considerable comfort in knowing that a loved one is being cared for physically, emotionally and spiritually, even if they cannot be physically present. Sometimes relatives will make the journey to see the dying person but arrive too late; or they arrive to find that the person they have come to see is likely to live longer than the length of their visit. We should be aware of how upsetting both of these situations can be.

Conclusion

Sheila Cassidy wrote that 'powerlessness and helplessness to prevent impending death' can be 'one of the hardest things for carers to come to terms with'.[3] Many loved ones express that they would do anything in order for the person not to be dying and leaving them, but are, of course, aware that they are helpless and power-

---

3 Sheila Cassidy, *Sharing the Darkness: The Spirituality of Caring* (London: Darton, Longman & Todd, 1988), p. 59.

less to do so. Sheila Cassidy writes of the need, in this situation, for a spirituality worked out 'at the foot of the cross'. This is the stance of the impotent bystander, just as Mary, Jesus' mother, kept vigil at the cross, completely powerless to do anything other than be there and witness her son die.[4]

When someone is dying, carers will often feel mixed emotions. It is not uncommon to hear a devoted partner or family member say, 'Does it sound awful that I just wished she would die now?' Reassurance that this is a common feeling, and that it can be an expression of kindness, can be a significant comfort. If the conversation turns to euthanasia, the information in Chapter 9 may be of use. Many carers are comforted by the reassurance that although doctors cannot and will not accelerate dying, equally it will not be artificially prolonged.

Regardless of the setting, many carers express a desire for privacy. The number of well-meaning visitors and professionals that come by can be overwhelming. One hospice chaplain recounted the story of being the gate-keeper in the case of a woman who meant well but whose frequent visits were tiring for the patient and interrupted time with the family.

In summary, looking after the holistic needs of carers is essential to good palliative care, not an 'add-on'. Moreover, the church visitor can play an important role here. Care of the carers, as with care of the dying, benefits from a team approach, involving shared responsibility and the work of helping one another through difficult situations.

How well a carer has been cared for will have a direct effect on the subsequent bereavement. Just as complex emotions can arise when carers perceive that their loved one was inadequately cared for or died an unnecessarily difficult death, so when they feel that no one listened to them or that they were 'left out of the loop'. Unanswered questions do not go away and they inhibit the ability to grieve and recover. Such experiences will also influence the approach that this person will have to the next death that he or she has to encounter. Supporters of assisted suicide sometimes

---

4 Cassidy, *Sharing the Darkness*, p. 59.

speak out of a painful memory of watching a loved one die an uncomfortable death, for which there seems no answers. Carers who have felt supported, however, tend to be able to look back and, alongside the pain of loss, find a sense of satisfaction that all was done that could have been done to help their loved one die well.

11

Children

Children dealing with death

Sitting in their school uniform, with the remnants of the day's lunch and paint over their shirt sleeves, you could easily believe that these two girls of eight and five years old had just experienced another 'normal' day at school. However, the truth was far from it. They had been picked up from school by their mother and driven to the hospice to see their father, who was terminally ill. That day he had taken a significant turn for the worse. The mother had been advised to bring the girls into the hospice, as no one was certain that he would last the night. She had been as honest as she could be with the girls from the very start of their father's illness, but she was not sure that they knew he was dying. Sioned was the doctor whose task was to talk with the girls, to check their under-standing. Of all the variety of pastorally demanding situations, explaining the facts of dying to young children is certainly among the most challenging.

We met in a very comfortable lounge in the hospice with the best chocolate biscuits we could find and some squash to drink. It was essential that Mum was also present, as a familiar comfort to the children. She had been keen for this encounter to occur. She and I had had a brief conversation beforehand, where she explained what she would like the girls to understand. We had agreed that she would start the conversation, as they would be much more responsive to her, as a safe, familiar person, than they would with a doctor they had never encountered before.

After an initial time of chatting about chocolate biscuits and school, the mother asked the girls if they knew why they had come to the hospice that evening. Snuggled into Mum's arms on either side, the younger one said, 'Daddy's not well'; the elder daughter just nodded.

I prayed that I would find the right words to express what needed to be said. I checked their understanding to date. Clearly, the girls were aware of their father's illness. Mum helped facilitate the conversation, to establish that they also knew that Daddy had received lots of medicine to try to make him better from his cancer. I was rapidly trying to assess the responses from these two girls, of different ages and clearly different personalities.

I kept trying to connect with Mum as unobtrusively as possible, to make sure that she wanted me to continue; her nods to me, through fought-back tears, suggested that it was important we did.

With strength that I could only attribute to the Holy Spirit, I explained that Dad had been so brave and had been amazing at taking all the medicines that had tried to make him better. I went on to say that sometimes, despite doctors and nurses doing everything they can, people do not get better. And sadly, Daddy was not going to get better.

Mum gained the confidence in that moment to say to the girls that it was time to say goodbye to Daddy, as he was going to be in heaven soon. They both cried, the reality of the situation having been put into words.

It was incredibly hard not to cry with them, but I sensed they needed me to be strong and to have some faith in the people looking after their father. After a few moments, I gently checked if there was anything they wanted to ask me. I imagined the confusion that must be going through their minds at that moment but equally was not surprised when they shook their heads. Mum nodded at me with an expression to say, 'That's enough'. I sensed they needed some time together, so I told them where I would be if they needed me and I got up to go. As I turned towards the door, the youngest said to me, 'Are there any more chocolate biscuits?' We of course obliged.

The story recounted here is based on a conglomerate of a few true stories, to protect the identity of those involved. It is intended to flag up several pertinent points.

We should not underestimate a child's understanding of a situation. Children are great observers, however hard we might work at hiding things to protect them. Honesty should be encouraged, otherwise children may imagine something very different is happening. The best person to talk to children is someone they love, respect and feel safe with, which is usually a close relative. The role of professional carers may best be one of facilitation, rather than taking the lead.

Charities all over the world have been set up to work with bereaved children. In the UK, the leading charity in this field is Winston's Wish. Their website is a fantastic resource for people working with children in this situation, or who are facing an imminent death. The charity provides information for children, parents and teachers. They recognize that children of different ages require different sorts of input, and that this can helpfully be presented in a variety of formats. They provide useful tips, dealing for instance with the language we might wish to use, and highlighting some of the terms that can add to the confusion, such as 'Granny has gone away' or 'We've lost Daddy'. There is also good literature available on how to talk to children about funerals.[1] Most experts would today encourage us to allow children to attend a funeral, rather than keeping them away.

Children may worry about things we have never considered, such as that cancer or another non-infectious disease is 'catching', or that they were somehow to blame for the illness. Usually these misunderstandings will come to the surface if a child is listened to carefully and trust is established. It is important to give children plenty of time and to seek to understand their perspective. We should not expect the dynamic to be only one way, either: a child's perspective on life and death can sometimes, even often, be a great source of hope.

Even in the face of very bad news, children often appear to carry on as though nothing were wrong. This can be disconcerting but is quite normal behaviour. We all find it difficult to remain

---

1 Michaelene Mundy, *What Happens When Someone Dies? A Child's Guide to Death and Funerals* (St Meinrad: Abbey Press, 2009).

CHILDREN

in a situation of sadness for too long, and that can be particularly true for a child. He or she may seem to be able to switch to
'normal' conversation quite swiftly, perhaps even by what looks
like a 'knight's move' to adults.

Dying children

Thanks to medical advances over the past decades, the death rate
for sick children in the developed world is much lower than it was
a century ago. To our shame, however, many children are still
dying in the developing world from reversible causes.

Most children requiring specialist palliative care in the West
will be those with a life-limiting condition, who are expected to
die in childhood. They may have been unwell for most, or all, of
their lives. Often the cause of illness is a degenerative condition,
a large proportion of which are genetic (or 'congenital'). Cancer
makes up a small percentage of those cared for in a children's
hospice.

The children's hospice movement in the UK started with Helen
House in Oxford, founded in 1982 by the All Saints' Sisters of the
Poor, a religious order in the Church of England.[2] Scotland's first
children's hospice, Rachel House, opened in 1996. There are now
40 children's hospice services around the UK; like adult hospices,
they receive very little government funding and rely heavily on
fundraising.

As with adults, the World Health Organization has provided a
definition of good palliative care for children:

Palliative care for children is the active total care of the child's
body, mind and spirit, and also involves giving support to the
family. It begins when illness is diagnosed, and continues regardless of whether or not a child receives treatment directed at the

2 The order was founded in 1851. Their vocation, in their own words, is 'to
be alongside the homeless and unemployed, the sick, the dying, the bereaved,
the old, the lonely – any who welcome the friendship we offer as companions
journeying together' <http://communities.anglicancommunion.org>.

disease. Health providers must evaluate and alleviate a child's physical, psychological, and social distress. Effective palliative care requires a broad multidisciplinary approach that includes the family and makes use of available community resources; it can be successfully implemented even if resources are limited. It can be provided in tertiary care facilities, in community health centres and even in children's homes.[3]

Families with a child with a life-limiting condition face a particularly traumatic situation and have particular needs, perhaps stretched over an extended period. There are many ways in which a minister or other member of a church can help. Studies have shown that relationships within families often suffer, that parents may rarely have a proper experience of mealtimes or a properly restful night's sleep. Some carers feel abandoned, and healthy siblings can feel left out. Social networks of friends frequently erode over time and formal respite is a scarce resource.

Children's hospices will therefore seek to provide services that offer a welcome oasis. In a typical children's hospice these will include:

- planned respite
- emergency respite
- a 24-hour telephone help line
- palliative care at hospice or home
- sibling support
- teenage weekends
- care at the time of death
- bereavement support.

Like adult hospices, a multi-disciplinary team will provide care for the child, along with care for siblings, and parents and grandparents. Most children's hospices have a chaplain whom they can

---

3 'WHO Definition of Palliative Care for Children' <www.who.int/cancer/palliative/definition/en/>.

call upon for spiritual support.[4] They also usually offer care on an out-patient basis, alongside periods when the child is admitted, with the hope that the condition can be stabilized and the child discharged, at least for a while. These aspects are particularly important when it comes to children with a terminal diagnosis. Beyond this, an outreach team will often offer to work with families in their own homes. A paediatric palliative care physician has drawn up a useful list for guidance in relation to dying children, as follows:[5]

Openness and willingness to engage in conversations between healthcare teams, children, and families about all options for care, including active treatment, palliative care, and their combination.

Equal understanding of and attention to physical, psychosocial and spiritual needs regardless of the care setting (home, hospital or hospice).

The right of children and families to choose their care setting and move freely between settings as needed.

The right of children and families to choose whom they wish to be present at the time of death.

Care that is consistent, compassionate, culturally sensitive and co-ordinated.

Care that is continuous through illness, dying, and bereavement.

4 In the UK, the Association of Hospice and Palliative Care Chaplains are currently forming a Children's Hospice Spiritual Care Network <www.ahpcc.org.uk/childrenshospice.html>.
5 Laura Beaune and Christine Newman, 'In search of a good death: Can children with life threatening illness and their families experience a good death?', *British Medical Journal*, 327 (2003), p. 222.

The death of a child

Pastoral visitors are sometimes asked to be involved with the care of a dying child and the child's family. This is a most challenging time for everyone involved. Care for other family members, especially siblings, is a vital part of what you can offer. A hospice may have a worker who can visit schools, where the effect of the death of a fellow pupil can be devastating.

The setting for this work may be a home, hospice or hospital. Initially disturbing though it might sound, when a child has died at home, use of a special 'refrigerated' bed has been found to be helpful for some families, as it allows a child's body to stay at home, in his own bedroom, until the time of the funeral, if the family prefer that to a funeral parlour.

Studies have also shown that, on reflection, most parents were glad that they had undertaken honest conversations with a sick child about death and dying. Most children will have ideas and opinions about what they would like to happen at their funeral, which is an important part of making sure that this day, of both sadness and celebration of a short life, will be one that reflects the child.

One of the key messages in this book is that care of the dying should never be a burden on a single person, and that no one need feel isolated and unsupported, and that includes lay, clergy and medical carers. If you find yourself in the situation of caring for a dying child, then do ask for help and support. As mentioned, many children's hospices will have a chaplain who is specially trained who can be called upon for assistance. Some children will die in hospital rather than at home or in a hospice; there will be hospital chaplains specifically assigned to the children's wards, and they too will be a great source of wisdom and knowledge.

12

After a Death

Legalities

Whenever someone dies, a death certificate is issued, following which there are clear legal requirements regarding the registration of the death. These will vary according to the law of each country.

Some patients will have expressed a wish to donate their organs after death. In the UK, the NHS Blood and Transplant Services have strict criteria regarding organ donation. For example, a patient who dies from advanced cancer may only be eligible to donate his or her corneas. Even then, there are certain requirements that not all patients will fulfil. If the patient is eligible, the Services organize the retrieval of the organ, which normally happens promptly. This does not delay the writing of the death certificate and there is no requirement for a coroner to be involved.[1]

Memorials

A terminal diagnosis may give friends and relatives time to say goodbye. In contrast, bereaved relatives of those who have died suddenly do not have the opportunity to say goodbye properly. Of course, a good leave-taking depends on the dying person

---

1 By and large, the churches see organ donation as an act of charity and therefore something to be encouraged. The practice, however, is not without moral difficulties on some occasions. A Christian may wish to ensure that organs are only removed *after death*, and to ensure that the carers enforce this wish, rather than having the removal of organs *cause death*, as can happen in some cases, in some countries.

having come to a place of acceptance and being herself able to experience the grief of losing what could have been. This is particularly difficult when children feature among those who will be bereaved, on a number of counts. For one, there is a natural fear that the children will forget about their relative who has died as they grow up. There is often a desire to leave something that can be a reminder of them in the future. One idea is to create something tangible such as a memory box to leave for children or grandchildren.

Suggesting this as an idea can be a difficult conversation to initiate, just as producing such an object can be an equally difficult task to complete. Many tears of joy and sadness are involved in building such a box but the creation of it in itself can bring with it a sense of healing.

A memory box is unique to each individual and will be filled with items that spark a special memory or a connection, for example between a child and his father who has died. It could be just a shoe box, or a handmade wooden box. Some ideas for filling a memory box include the following; this list is by no means exhaustive.

- photographs
- a CD of music that has particular significance
- a DVD recording a message of love or recounting special family moments
- a letter
- poetry
- a picture or crafted object of significance
- perfume or aftershave, as the smell will trigger memories
- a lock of hair
- an item of clothing or jewellery.

It is helpful to let at least one other family member or close friend know where the box is. They can also have a role in helping the child to remember and in filling in any gaps. Information about memory boxes can be found on the Winston's Wish website.

Funerals and visiting

After a death comes a funeral, and a funeral conducted well can be an important part of the grieving process; it is a highly significant part of what the Church offers the bereaved. A 'good funeral' is likely to be one based on some careful preparation, not least in terms of getting to know the family and the story of the person who has died. If the minister, or a member of a congregation, has been involved in care while the person was dying, those bonds and informed sense of the person are already in place. In any case, the minister will want to spend some time with the bereaved family before the funeral, discussing the service and the life of the person who has died.

The form and feel of funeral services will vary from tradition to tradition, but a 'good funeral' is likely to integrate elements that are highly personal with other elements that are more formally liturgical and set down in a prayer book. Perhaps never more than at a funeral, we see that the distillation of wisdom found in liturgical texts can speak to us profoundly, and set our feelings and the particular situation we face within a larger context. Alongside individual texts, we encounter this wisdom and theological perspective in the structure of the service and the sense of what should be included as a minimum, whatever else we may wish to add.

A continuing part of our care for a dying person and their relatives and friends is to be alongside the mourners as they organize a funeral. Of course, this may not be the first time that the subject of the funeral has come up. Many dying people talk through their wishes before they die. The minister conducting the funeral will usually be from the church with which the dying person was associated, if they were. This is most often the local church, for instance, in the Church of England parish in which they lived. If the deceased or the relatives want the service to be conducted by a particular minister, or for the funeral to be in a particular church, they should make this clear to the funeral directors. It is best not to settle on a date or time until the minister in question has been contacted.

When it comes to choosing a funeral director, it is good to

have a personal recommendation. Another thing to look for is membership of a professional body. (In the UK, that would be the National Association of Funeral Directors or the Society of Allied and Independent Funeral Directors.) Most directors work by the highest professional standards. A personal recommendation and membership of a professional body will help to sift out, and avoid, the very occasional rogue who can let the side down.

Almost all churches are comfortable with both burial and cremation. The latter used sometimes to be met with disapproval, in case it constituted a tacit rejection of the resurrection of the dead. In reality, our mortal remains are eventually dissipated, whichever route is taken, and that is not seen as mitigating the belief that God will raise the dead to new life, with restored and glorious bodies.

Part of a response to a death usually involves planning a memorial, to mark the place where a body has been buried or ashes have been interred. There may not be a memorial if ashes are scattered; this lack of a tangible marker or sense of laying remains to rest in hope of the resurrection are good reasons for interring ashes rather than scattering them.

In most church jurisdictions, a proposal for the memorial needs to be approved before it can be erected, either for a municipal graveyard or a parish burial ground. The rules are more restrictive for Church of England graveyards than for municipal ones, for the very reason that makes the graveyards attractive: the setting is likely to be particularly historical and picturesque, and any new memorial will have to be in keeping with the historical character of the setting. Very occasionally, a stonemason will proceed with a memorial without telling the family that permission has to be sought, and this can lead to the distressing situation where a memorial has been made, and paid for, but cannot be put in place.

Ongoing care of the bereaved is as much part of the work of the Church as care of the dying. Among the frustrations likely to be expressed by clergy is a sense that time does not allow them to follow up bereavements with anything like the frequency or individual care that they would like. Pastoral care, of course, is not the sole preserve of the clergy, and bereavement visiting is one of the most immediately useful things that a church lay pastoral visitors scheme can take under its wings. Some general pastoral training is highly advisable, as is some specific training in working with the bereaved. Ultimately, however, a church visitor is most of all going to be offering time, concern and attention, a listening ear and some sensible human and Christian advice, rather than being a fully trained counsellor. If a bereaved person is facing a particularly prolonged or agonized bereavement it is good to know when to suggest that they might turn to more highly trained help. In the UK, the first port of call may well be the bereavement counselling charity Cruse.

Word should also be said about safeguarding, the law and good practice. The people most likely to be a priority for a visiting scheme will be those who are most in need, and the more someone is in need, the more likely that they will fall into the category of 'vulnerable adult'. Definitions vary, and indeed different organizations may have their own slightly different definitions of what makes an adult vulnerable. The Diocese of Guildford, for example, defines a vulnerable adult as: 'A person aged 18 or over, who is, or may be, in need of community care services by reason of mental or other disability, age or illness; and who is, or may be, unable to take care of him or herself, or unable to protect him or herself against significant harm or exploitation.'[2] Anyone wishing to visit a person falling into this category would have to be vetted by the national body responsible for checking criminal records (now the Disclosure and Barring Service, previously the Criminal Records Bureau). It is therefore sensible, and may even be necessary, that any church bereavement visitor has such a check, just as we would expect for a Sunday school helper, for instance.

Other schemes for following up pastoral care after a bereavement could be considered. They can run parallel to visiting, rather than replacing it. Many churches hold a memorial service or requiem once per year, perhaps around All Souls' Day (2 November), or more often. Prayers might be said for the bereaved, and

2 <http://cofeguildford.org.uk/assets/downloads/departments/safeguarding andinclusion/safeguardinghandbook.pdf>.

for the deceased in many traditions, for a number of Sundays after a death, or at a daily service. A card could be sent to let the bereaved know about this. Some will want to come, in order to hear and take part; others will be comforted to know that the church is praying for them. If the dead and bereaved are remembered at the anniversary of a death (sometimes called the 'year's mind'), a card could, again, let the family know.

Finally, an invitation to church social events is often useful and can be highly significant. Bereavement can leave mourners feeling cut off, especially if someone is left a widow or widower. Coming to social events, some of which might happen regularly every week, is likely to provide a great deal more ongoing social contact, and opportunity for friendship, than the perhaps no more than quarterly visit from the clergy, or even the most assiduous lay pastoral visiting team.

Conclusion

As we come to the conclusion of this book, we hope that the reader has found it useful as part of the preparation for work with the dying, or perhaps that it has offered something by way of refreshment to those already involved with this ministry of the Church.

Although you may come to refer to this book again in the future, remembering details of this or that medical or theological point does not lie at the heart of what makes for good care of the dying. That lies in who-one-is, rather than in what-one-knows. Each of us has, in our common humanity and in our Christian faith, all that we most profoundly need to accompany those whose lives are drawing to an end.

A few points may be worth recalling by way of summary. Communication lies at the heart of what we are doing in this work. That does not necessarily mean being able to find just the right words. If we approach those who are dying out of a motivation of compassion, we are unlikely to go far wrong.

Good care for the dying is responsive to the needs of the whole person. This chimes with the sense in Christian teaching that we are both bodily and spiritual, that we are valuable as individuals, and also inherently social, that we are rational and feeling, that we are rooted in both geography and history, and so on. When it comes to being with a dying person, nothing is simply, reductively and *only* medical, material or physical. Similarly, our most profound spiritual needs are worked out in relation to the body, the family and friends, and physical needs. Sometimes what matters most may be as mundane as making sure that the cat is fed or that bills are paid.

This is part of what it means for palliative care to be *holistic*, or attending to the whole. That holism means that relatives are included in the provision of care, alongside the patient; it also means that those who look after the dying need to look after themselves. Holism prompts the welcome observation that care of the dying is almost always now seen as requiring a team approach. That team takes in professionals and volunteers, family and friends, medics, clergy, church visitors and others. No one should feel alone or isolated in this ministry; no serious decision should be taken without consultation.

The many ways in which clergy and pastoral visitors can contribute to this holistic care have been explored, although the suggestions here are only a beginning. The opportunities for churches and concerned Christians to contribute to the care of the dying are many and varied. It is almost certainly best to concentrate on what is most feasible and what most suits the gifts of those who are involved. Even those opportunities that lie close at hand are often relatively under-explored in many parishes and similar settings. An 'audit' may be a useful exercise, where a congregation considers what it might do in this area.

Alongside such practical stocktaking, we can think about the place of death in our teaching and common reflection. Many churches and preachers do not address the subject of death at all often. Similarly, care of the elderly, sick and dying can be given second place to projects that are directed to the young, just as attention can be shifted away from the traditional pastoral mission of the Church to new initiatives.

Beyond the life of individual churches, Christians also have a place in shaping national debate about the care of those in the last stages of life. This takes in emotive topics, such as euthanasia. They are no less significant for being emotive. Less arresting, but hugely important, is the task of extending the provision of excellent palliative care for all. Indeed, these two topics are related. The call for assisted suicide and euthanasia will be countered just as effectively by provision of the best medical and pastoral care as they will by intellectual arguments, if not more so. The best way to uphold the sanctity of life in law is to uphold the sanctity of life in practice.

Beyond the affluent West, even the basics of good pain control can be lacking. As much as we attend to the needs of our own cultures, Christians have a role to play in imagining a world where all who are dying have access to good care at the end of life, regardless of where they live or what disease they have.

In any case, and in every place, we might do well to remember the example of Dame Cicely Saunders, whose work and life have punctuated this book. Everything she did expressed her determination that 'We will do all we can not only to help you die peacefully but also to live until you die.'[1] We can all contribute to this goal.

---

1 Cicely Saunders with an Introduction by David Clark, *Cicely Saunders: Selected Writings 1958–2004* (Oxford: Oxford University Press, 2006), p. 257.

Appendix: Prayers for Use with the Dying

The Christian tradition provides some excellent prayers and devotions to use with those who are dying. Two particularly well-loved texts sometimes go by their Latin names: *Anima Christi* ('Soul of my Saviour') and *Proficiscere, anima Christiana* ('Go forth, Christian soul').

Anima Christi

Soul of Christ, sanctify me.
Body of Christ, save me.
Blood of Christ, refresh me.
Water from the side of Christ, wash me.
Passion of Christ, strengthen me.
O good Jesus, hear me.
Within your wounds hide me.
Let me never be separated from you.
From the power of darkness defend me.
In the hour of my death, call me
and bid me come to you,
that with your saints I may praise you
for ever and ever. Amen.[1]

---

1 Sometimes attributed to Pope John XXII, early fourteenth century. Translator unknown.

Proficiscere, anima Christiana

[*Name*], go forth upon your journey from this world,
in the name of God the Father almighty who created you;
in the name of Jesus Christ who suffered death for you;
in the name of the Holy Spirit who strengthens you;
in communion with the blessed saints
and aided by angels and archangels,
and all the armies of the heavenly host.
May your portion this day be in peace,
and your dwelling the heavenly Jerusalem. Amen.[2]

A helpful collection, or style, of prayers for use with people close
to death are those written for use at the close of the day. Alongside individual texts, this includes the set (or 'office') of prayers
called Night Prayer or Compline. This service is much loved by
many who have encountered it.

'The Lord Almighty grant us a quiet night, and a perfect end',
it often begins, thereby already connecting death with sleep. That
connection goes back, in fact, to what is probably the earliest book
of the New Testament: 1 Thessalonians, where Paul refers to the
dead as 'those who have fallen asleep' (1 Thess. 4.13).[3] Our word
cemetery also bears witness to this connection: it comes from the
Latin *coemeterium* (and that from the Greek *koimeterion*) meaning 'sleeping place or dormitory'. Christians were the first to apply
that word to the location of burial.

One of the collects associated with Compline, at least in the
Church of England, puts this well. It addresses Christ,

who at this evening hour lay in the tomb
and so hallowed the grave
to be a bed of hope for all who put their trust in you.

---

2 Translation from *Common Worship: Pastoral Services* (London: Church
House Publishing, 2000).
3 The literal meaning of the Greek is given only in a footnote by the NRSV.

With that in mind, we might make use of the whole of Compline with the dying, or part of it, such as this collect.

> Almighty God,
> by triumphing over the powers of darkness
> Christ has prepared a place for us in the new Jerusalem:
> may we, who [... give] thanks for his resurrection,
> praise him in the eternal city
> of which he is the light;
> through Jesus Christ our Lord.

Or this refrain:

> Grant us your light, O Lord,
> that the darkness of our hearts being overcome,
> we may receive the true light,
> even Christ our Saviour.

Finally, here is an eighth-century hymn sung at Compline during Lent:

> O Christ, who art the Light and Day,
> thou drivest darksome night away:
> we know thee as the Light of light
> illuminating mortal sight.

> All holy Lord, we pray to thee,
> keep us tonight from danger free:
> grant us, dear Lord, in thee to rest;
> so be our sleep in quiet blessed.

> And while the eyes soft slumber take,
> still be the heart to thee awake,
> be thy right hand upheld above
> thy servants resting in thy love.

Yea, our Defender, be thou nigh,
to bid the powers of darkness fly;
keep us from sin, and guide for good
thy servants purchased by thy blood.

Remember us, dear Lord, we pray,
while in this mortal flesh we stay:
'tis thou who dost the soul defend;
be present with us to the end.[4]

---

4 *Christe qui lux es et dies.* Translated by William John Copeland and others, from the *English Hymnal* (Oxford: Oxford University Press, 1906). The doxology has been omitted as it has a specifically Lenten reference.

Bibliography

Pastoral care and bereavement

Ian Ainsworth-Smith and Peter Speck, *Letting Go: Caring for the Dying and Bereaved* (London: SPCK, 1999). Written by hospital chaplains.

Mitch Albom, *Tuesdays with Morrie: An Old Man, a Young Man and Life's Greatest Lesson* (New York: Doubleday, 1997). Mitch Albom is reunited with his college professor Morrie Schwartz, who is dying from ALS/MND. He teaches Mitch some of life's most important lessons.

Shirley du Boulay and Marianne Rankin, *Cicely Saunders: The Founder of the Modern Hospice Movement* (London: SPCK, 2007).

Maggie Callanan and Patricia Kelley, *Final Gifts: Understanding the Special Awareness, Needs and Communications of the Dying* (London: Hodder & Stoughton, 1992). Written by two hospice nurses who share their experience of working with patients at the end of life.

Sheila Cassidy, *Sharing the Darkness: The Spirituality of Caring* (London: Darton, Longman & Todd, 1988). Cassidy shares her experiences of work with the dying and explores our shared humanity in face of suffering, blending it with reflections on the Gospels.

Christopher Chapman, *Seeing in the Dark: Pastoral Perspectives on Suffering from the Christian Spiritual Tradition* (London: Canterbury Press, 2013).

M. Cobb, *The Dying Soul: Spiritual Care at the End of Life* (Oxford: Oxford University Press, 2001). Cobb's book stresses the importance of 'spiritual care' alongside physical, psychological and social care as part of a holistic approach. The perspective draws on various faith traditions.

Ralph Crawshaw, *Compassion's Way: A Doctor's Quest into the Soul of Medicine* (Bloomington, IN: Medi-ed Press, 2002). This is a compilation of experiences by a sensitive American physician in his search for compassion in medicine and in the wider world.

Andrew Davison, *Why Sacraments?* (London: SPCK, 2013). One of the authors of this book explores the place of the sacraments in the Christian life, and the theology behind them, including the sacraments given to the sick.

Joan Didion, *The Year of Magical Thinking* (London: Vintage, 2007). This great wordsmith gives a haunting account of the first year of bereavement.

Abigail Rian Evans, *Is God Still at the Bedside?: The Medical, Ethical and Pastoral Issues of Death and Dying* (Grand Rapids, MI: Eerdmans, 2010). The author, a retired professor of practical theology from the United States, offers a multi-disciplinary approach, taking in medical, theological, legal, ethical and pastoral disciplines surrounding death and dying, written from an American Christian perspective.

Marie Fallon and Geoffrey Hanks (eds), *ABC of Palliative Care* (Oxford: British Medical Journal Books, 2006). This was written with medical personnel in mind, but accessibly so. It contains a wealth of contributions from some of the current leaders in the field. It is disappointing that it has no contribution from a chaplain, or chapter on spiritual care.

J. F. Hanratty, *Care of the Dying: Philosophy of Terminal Illness* (Hackney: St Joseph's Hospice, 1987). This booklet was written by one of the former medical directors of St Joseph's Hospice in London. It covers principles of the care of the dying with emphasis on communication, love and care. The principles hold 25 years on.

Elisabeth Kübler-Ross, *On Death and Dying: What the Dying have to Teach Doctors, Nurses, Clergy and their own Families*, with Introduction by Professor Allan Kellehear (London: Routledge, 2008). An anniversary edition of a seminal text, first published in 1969. It was one of the first works to look at bereavement. Her stages of grief have since been further explored and adapted.

C. S. Lewis, *A Grief Observed* (London: Faber and Faber, 1961).

Anne Long, *Listening* (London: Darton, Longman & Todd, 1990). An easily readable book looking at how we listen to God, ourselves and others.

Anne Merriman, *Audacity to Love: The Story of Hospice Africa* (Irish Hospice Foundation, 2010). This is an inspirational account of Dr Merriman's pioneering achievements in setting up Hospice Africa to bring much-needed palliative care to that continent. Alongside many challenges, she learns a great deal in that setting.

Barbara Monroe and David Oliviere, *Resilience in Palliative Care: Achievement in Adversity* (Oxford: Oxford University Press, 2007).

Michaelene Mundy, *What Happens When Someone Dies? A Child's Guide to Death and Funerals* (St Meinrad: Abbey Press, 2009). An illustrated book, part of a series written to help children with grief and loss. It talks about God and assumes the concept of life after death.

Derek Murray, *Faith in Hospices: Spiritual Care and the End of Life* (London: SPCK, 2002). Murray draws on his long experience as chaplain at St Colomba's Hospice in Edinburgh in a way that models good pastoral care. The focus is on hospice care, and he speaks candidly about the realities of death and some of the limitations of the hospice movement. The chapters end with questions that promote thought for study.

Roger Neighbour, *The Inner Consultation* (Lancaster: Radcliffe, 2005) and *The Inner Apprentice* (Lancaster: Radcliffe, 2004). These books look at different models of communication within a consultation, suggesting structures for doctors, through which to engage effectively with patients. They are useful for the non-physician.

Julia Neuberger, *Caring for Dying People of Different Faiths* (Abingdon: Radcliffe Medical Press, 2004.)

Julia Neuberger, *Dying Well: A Guide to Enabling a Good Death* (Oxford: Radcliffe Publishing, 2004). Here Neuberger looks at how different cultures, religions and philosophical standpoints view death. The book also covers the hospice movement, euthanasia, living wills and advance directives.

The Roman Catholic Bishops' Conference of England and Wales, *A Practical Guide to the Spiritual Care of the Dying Person* (London: Catholic Truth Society, 2010).

Cicely Saunders, *Cicely Saunders: Selected Writings – 1958–2004*, Introduction by David Clark (Oxford: Oxford University Press, 2006).

Jonathan Silverman, Suzanne M. Kurtz and Juliet Draper, *Skills for Communicating with Patients* (Oxford: Radcliffe, 2005). This covers similar territory to Roger Neighbour's books.

John Swinton and Richard Payne, *Living Well and Dying Faithfully: Christian Practices for End of Life Care* (Grand Rapids, MI: Eerdmans, 2009). These authors offer a provocation to think about what it means to do medicine in a theological context rather than theology in a medical context.

Jennifer Tan (ed.), *Soul Pain: Priests Reflect on Personal Experiences of Serious and Terminal Illness* (London: Canterbury Press, 2013). A highly relevant collection of essays for those working with the dying.

Robert G. Twycross, *Introducing Palliative Care* (Abingdon: Radcliffe Medical Press, 2002). A classic text, used primarily by health professionals in the field, with large sections devoted to the medical management of symptoms and reference to spiritual care. The medical terminology narrows the readership to those familiar with this vocabulary.

Max Watson, Caroline Lucas, Andrew Hoy and Jo Wells, *Oxford Handbook of Palliative Care* (Oxford: Oxford University Press, 2009). For anyone involved in the field of palliative care, this is a good reference book.

Jacqueline Worswick, *A House Called Helen: The Story of the First Hospice for Children* (London: HarperCollins, 1993).

Theology

Philippe Ariès was the principal cultural historian of death in the late twentieth century. His books include *Images of Man and Death*, trans. Janet Lloyd (Cambridge, MA: Harvard University Press, 1985), *The Hour of Our Death*, trans. Helen Weaver (New York: Alfred A. Knopf, 1981) and *Western Attitudes toward Death: From the Middle Ages to the Present*, trans. Patricia M. Ranum (Baltimore, MD: Johns Hopkins University Press, 1974).

Caroline Walker Bynum, *The Resurrection of the Body in Western Christianity, 200–1336* (New York: Columbia University Press, 1996). A study from one of the great theological cultural historians.

Douglas James Davies, *A Brief History of Death* (Oxford: Blackwell, 2004).

Douglas James Davies, *The Theology of Death* (Edinburgh: T&T Clark, 2007).

David Albert Jones, *Approaching the End: A Theological Exploration of Death and Dying* (Oxford: Oxford University Press, 2007). This book is particularly recommended.

Peter Jupp, *Death Our Future: Christian Theology and Funeral Practice* (London: Epworth, 2008).

Fergus Kerr, *Immortal Longings: Versions of Transcending Humanity* (London: SPCK, 1997). Kerr looks at various, mainly philosophical, discussions of 'transcendence': how this world relates to something beyond it.

Eric Mascall, *Grace and Glory* (London: Faith Press, 1961). Mascall's short book is a beautiful meditation on the life of the world to come, and draws upon the theological tradition, not least from St Augustine.

Terence Nichols, *Death and Afterlife: A Theological Introduction* (Grand Rapids, MI: Brazos Press, 2010).

Josef Pieper, 'Hope', in *Faith, Hope, Love*, trans. Richard Winston, Clara Winston and Frances McCarthy (San Francisco: Ignatius, 1986). Pieper wrote as perceptively on the virtues as anyone else in the twentieth century.

Janet Soskice, 'Dying Well in Christianity' in Harold Coward and Kelli I. Stajduhar (eds), *Religious Understandings of a Good Death in Hospice Palliative Care* (Albany: State University of New York Press, 2012).

Darlene Fozard Weaver, 'Death' in Gilbert Meilaender and William Werpehowski (eds), *The Oxford Handbook of Theological Ethics* (Oxford: Oxford University Press, 2005).

Tom Wright, *Surprised by Hope: Rethinking Heaven, the Resurrection, and the Mission of the Church* (London: SPCK, 2007). Wright has done much to put the resurrection of Christ, and the general resurrection, back at the centre of Christian thought. Here he is writing in his clear and accessible mode.

Two classics from previous centuries on preparation for death are Jeremy Taylor, *The Rule and Exercises of Holy Dying* and Robert Bellarmine, *The Art of Dying Well*. Both are available in many editions.

Two theologians have written theological reflections on their own loss of a child: Nicholas Wolterstorff, *Lament for a Son* (Grand Rapids, MI: Eerdmans, 1987) and John De Gruchy, *Led into Mystery: Faith Seeking Answers in Life and Death* (London: SCM Press, 2013).

Bible Index

Name Index

Subject Index